ADRENALINE RUSH

FLIX FOR GUYS

GROUP'S

DINNER *A* MOVIE

Friendship, Faith, and Fun for **Guys' Groups**

Group

Loveland, Colorado ®

www.group.com

Group

Group resources actually work!

This Group resource helps you focus on **"The 1 Thing"®**—a life-changing relationship with Jesus Christ. "The 1 Thing" incorporates our **R.E.A.L.** approach to ministry. It reinforces a growing friendship with Jesus, encourages long-term learning, and results in life transformation, because it's:

Relational
Learner-to-learner interaction enhances learning and builds Christian friendships.

Experiential
What learners experience through discussion and action sticks with them up to 9 times longer than what they simply hear or read.

Applicable
The aim of Christian education is to equip learners to be both hearers and doers of God's Word.

Learner-based
Learners understand and retain more when the learning process takes into consideration how they learn best.

Group's Dinner and a Movie: Adrenaline Rush
Copyright © 2008 Group Publishing, Inc.

Visit our Web site: **www.group.com**

Credits
Contributing Authors: Brian Diede, Mikal Keefer, Tony Nappa, Owen Shattuck, Thomas Smith, Michael van Schooneveld, Jeff White
Editor: Ann Marie Rozum
Senior Developer: Amy Nappa
Project Manager: Scott M. Kinner
Chief Creative Officer: Joani Schultz
Copy Editor: Dena Twinem
Art Director: Jeff Storm
Print Production Artist: YaYe Design
Cover Art Director: Jeff Storm
Cover Designer: Jeff Storm
Illustrator: Matt Wood
Production Manager: DeAnne Lear

Unless otherwise noted, Scripture taken from the *HOLY BIBLE*, NEW INTERNATIONAL VERSION®. Copyright © 1973, 1978, 1984 by International Bible Society. Used by permission of Zondervan Publishing House. All rights reserved.

Library of Congress Cataloging-in-Publication Data

Group's dinner and a movie : adrenaline rush : friendship, faith, and
fun for guys / [contributing authors, Brian Diede ... et al.]. – 1st
American pbk. ed.
     p. cm.
  ISBN 978-0-7644-3710-6 (pbk. : alk. paper) 1. Church work with men.
2. Church group work. 3. Motion pictures in church work. 4.
Cookery–Religious aspects–Christianity. I. Diede, Brian.
  BV4440.G76 2008
  259.081–dc22

                              2007038349

ISBN 978-0-7644-3710-6

Printed in the United States of America.
10 9 8 7 6 5 4 3 2 1   17 16 15 14 13 12 11 10 09 08

TABLE OF CONTENTS

INTRODUCTION 4

Batman Begins 5

Star Wars 12

Miracle 19

Raiders of the Lost Ark 26

The Incredibles 33

Signs 40

Galaxy Quest 47

The Exorcism of Emily Rose 54

Apollo 13 61

What About Bob? 68

The Lord of the Rings:
  The Fellowship of the Ring 75

The Bourne Identity 82

X-Men 88

Escape From Alcatraz 95

I, Robot 102

INVITATIONS 109

# INTRODUCTION

Welcome to *Group's Dinner and a Movie: Adrenaline Rush*,
a resource for men who really love food and movies!

During these out-of-the-ordinary small-group events, you'll cook a meal together with the guys, and you'll get into lively discussions around the dinner table (TalkStarters are included with each event). Then you'll watch a movie together as you munch on snacks. Afterward you'll discuss the spiritual themes of the movie.

There's something about shared time in the kitchen—or at the grill—and then a shared meal together that really increases the dynamics of fellowship within a group of friends. As you chop, stir, cook, eat, and joke around together, you'll learn about each other and build relationships that will last a lifetime. In short, you'll learn to be a community. Isn't that just what God wants for your church?

Not only that, but there's much to learn about ourselves and God in the movies. We'll watch stories of disobedience, betrayal, regret, and revenge. We'll also witness love, sacrifice, grace, and redemption. All of these themes, played out in a variety of dramas, comedies, adventure stories (and even a relevant horror flick), can powerfully teach men about the God we serve and how to follow him more. Besides that, watching these movies with an eye toward the spiritual will help men look for God in every movie or TV show they watch.

Sometimes, though, movies that encourage the most profound or insightful discussions are those that some might consider gritty or even mildly offensive. For that reason, though we obviously recommend the films we've included in this book, **we strongly urge you to preview each movie before playing it for your friends.**

These events are great anytime. They're perfect to use for a guys' night out or a fellowship evening or for that lull when you're between studies. You can have a Dinner and a Movie once a quarter, once a month, or anytime your group wants to get together for something out of the ordinary.

We hope you enjoy these Dinner and a Movie events! Start the show!

Is It Legal to Show These Movies to My Small Group?

In general, federal copyright laws do allow you to use videos or DVDs for the purpose of home viewing as long as you aren't charging admission. However, you may feel more comfortable if you purchase a license. Your church can obtain a license from Christian Video Licensing International for a small fee. Just visit www.cvli.org or call 1-888-302-6020 for more information. When using a movie that is not covered by the license, we recommend directly contacting the production company to seek permission to use it.

THE MOVIE

BATMAN BEGINS

Genre: Action **Length:** 140 minutes **Rating:** PG-13

Quick Plot: Bruce Wayne travels the world seeking to fight injustice, a journey that will ultimately result in his transformation into the Dark Knight.

Why This Movie Is Great for Guys: Justice-dealing superheroes! Bruce Wayne's struggle with fear and his lust for vengeance will prompt men to evaluate how they handle their own fears and to examine the concept of justice.

 Note: This movie is rated PG-13 for intense action violence, disturbing images, and certain thematic elements.

FOOD

Ninja's Pocket of Deadly [Good] Chicken
Falcone's Breadsticks
Billionaire Soda
Drinks (water, tea)
Mr. Freeze's Chocolate Cherries

THE FOOD

Before your event, talk to the guys about dividing up the ingredients and supplies. Keep in mind that some items, such as the chicken, cost a lot more than others. Maybe two people could share the cost of the chicken while others each bring a couple of items.

What you'll need: Names:

Ninja's Pocket of Deadly [Good] Chicken (serves 8)

2 pounds chicken meat

1 bag frozen stir-fry vegetables

⅔ cup shredded cabbage (red)

4 tablespoons soy sauce

1 tablespoon oyster sauce (optional)

½ teaspoon five-spice powder

2 tablespoons peanut or
    vegetable oil

1 head iceberg lettuce

Falcone's Breadsticks (serves 8)

1 precooked pizza crust, such
    as Boboli

1½ tablespoons olive oil

1 teaspoon garlic powder

¼ cup grated or shredded
    Parmesan cheese

1 jar or tub marinara sauce
    for dipping

Billionaire Soda (serves 8-10)

2 liter bottle ginger ale

1 cup grapefruit juice

½ cup orange juice

4 tablespoons grenadine or
    pomegranate juice

Drinks (water, tea)

Mr. Freeze's Chocolate Cherries (recipe on page 8)

Easy Option Meal

If your group doesn't feel like doing much cooking, pick up a frozen lasagna (try vegetarian or chicken for a change) at the supermarket, some frozen garlic bread, and a bottle of sparkling cider.

You remembered the food—but don't forget napkins, plates, and silverware. Amaze (amuse?) your guests with Batman paper goods from your local discount store, or use paper Japanese-style square plates for a sophisticated ninja vibe.

Ninja's Pocket of Deadly [Good] Chicken

2 pounds chicken meat (white or dark), chopped
1 bag frozen stir-fry vegetables
⅔ cup shredded cabbage (red preferred)
4 tablespoons soy sauce

1 tablespoons oyster sauce (optional)
½ teaspoon five-spice powder
2 tablespoons peanut or vegetable oil
1 fresh head iceberg lettuce

Thaw the frozen vegetables overnight in the fridge. Heat the oil in a wok over medium-high heat. Add the chicken and cook, stirring constantly, for about 3 minutes, until chicken is nearly cooked. Add the cabbage and vegetables and stir-fry for one minute. Add the soy sauce, oyster sauce (optional), and five-spice powder and stir-fry for one to two minutes, until veggies are tender and the sauces have combined. Tear off several lettuce leaves together and place one serving of chicken mixture into each group of lettuce leaves, as if it were a bowl. Serves 8.

Falcone's Breadsticks

1 precooked pizza crust, such as Boboli
1½ tablespoons olive oil
1 teaspoon garlic powder

¼ cup grated or shredded Parmesan cheese
1 jar or tub marinara sauce for dipping

Preheat your oven to 350 degrees. Brush the pizza crust with oil and sprinkle with garlic powder and Parmesan cheese. Partially cut the crust into breadstick shapes by cutting several long lines down it and two across; try not to cut all the way through. Bake for 5-10 minutes or until golden and remove. Separate the sticks and serve with warm marinara. Serves 8.

Billionaire Soda

2 liter bottle ginger ale
1 cup grapefruit juice
½ cup orange juice

4 tablespoons grenadine or pomegranate juice

Chill ginger ale. Mix and serve in tumblers or champagne glasses. Proclaim toasts that you think Bruce Wayne might give. Serves 8-10.

Mr. Freeze's Chocolate Cherries

½ bag frozen, pitted Bing cherries   ½ bag chocolate chips (about 6 oz)

Melt the chocolate in a microwave safe bowl or in a double boiler, stirring frequently. Dip each cherry in the chocolate, thoroughly coating it, and place on a sheet of wax paper to harden. Let stand for about 10-15 minutes, then eat, or put on a plate and refrigerate for later. Serves 8.

GETTING READY FOR THE SHOW

TalkStarters
Use these questions to prompt discussions as you eat together:
• If you could be any comic book hero, which would you be? Why?
• When you were young, who was your hero? In what ways have you tried to emulate that person?
• Tell about a childhood fear. How've you overcome that fear?
• What is currently one of your greatest fears? What do you do to combat this fear?
• Have you ever "taken the law into your own hands," in any sense? What happened?

Batman Trivia Quiz
1. What city does Batman live in?
    A. Metropolis
    B. New York
    C. Gotham
2. What superpowers does Batman have?
3. What crime-fighting team has Batman often been a part of?
4. What is the name of Bruce Wayne's butler?
5. How many of Batman's greatest enemies can you name?
6. Who was the first actor to portray Batman on film?
7. (Extra Credit) Bats account for about what percentage of all mammal species?
    A. 1%
    B. 15%
    C. 20%

Answers
1. C. Gotham
2. None. He's simply extremely fit, incredibly intelligent, and very rich.
3. The Justice League
4. Alfred
5. The Joker, The Penguin, Two-Face, Poison Ivy, Mr. Freeze, Catwoman, The Riddler, Scarecrow, Bane
6. Not Michael Keaton in 1989, or Adam West in 1966, but Lewis Wilson in 1943!
7. C. 20% There are over a 1,000 species of bats worldwide. Of those, most eat only insects, and the rest subsist primarily on fruit and juices. Only three species drink blood, and none fight crime.

Making Dinner Happen

You have the home-court advantage here, so make it easy on yourself and have a cooking plan in mind before the event (decide how you'll assign tasks for meal prep). Then, when guests arrive, distribute photocopied recipes and have everyone work together to get the food on the table.

SHOWTIME!

The Pre-Show

Have everyone gather in the area where you'll show the movie. If you've just finished eating, you may want to provide a quick break for people to use the rest room. Take a few moments before you start to raise your glasses of Billionaire Soda and have each person name a toast to one of their heroes. Serve the chocolate cherries and more soda when the movie gets to the part where Bruce boards the airplane to return home.

THE SHOW

Genre: Action

Length: 140 minutes

Rating: PG-13 for intense action violence (shootings, fights) and disturbing images (psychological torture, delusions)

Plot: Bruce Wayne grows up with the proverbial silver spoon in his mouth, but despite inherited wealth his life unravels after a tragic event. When his parents are murdered, Bruce loses himself to his fears and his desire for vengeance. He leaves his home city of Gotham—frustrated and unable to cope—and seeks understanding amid the dark hollows of the criminal underworld.

When a society of vigilantes takes Bruce under their wing to train him, he realizes that there's more to justice than raw vengeance. With a new sense of purpose, Bruce returns to Gotham to rid the city of crime and to make a new name for himself as Batman, the Dark Knight.

The story doesn't end here, though. Bruce must still deal with the loose threads and problems he left behind. Not only is the city caught in the grip of a criminal kingpin; Batman is secretly threatened by an enemy from his past—one with a deadly plan to destroy the very minds of the people of Gotham. It seems impossible for one man to make a difference, but Bruce is determined to be more than just a man...

Just for Fun!

Got a few extra minutes? Quiz everyone on the following *Batman Begins* movie quotes.

WHO SAID:

- *"Why do we fall, Bruce? So we can learn to pick ourselves up."*
  (Thomas Wayne)

- *"I seek a means to fight injustice, to turn fear against those who prey on the fearful."*
  (Bruce Wayne)

- *"Do I look like a cop?"*
  (Bruce Wayne)

- *"All creatures feel fear. Especially the scary ones."*
  (Thomas Wayne)

- *"Justice is harmony. Revenge is about you making yourself feel better."*
  (Rachel Dawes)

- *"Your compassion is a weakness your enemies will not share." "That's why it's so important; it separates us from them."*
  (Henri Ducard, Bruce Wayne)

- *"Gentlemen. Time to spread the word. And the word is—panic."*
  (Henri Ducard)

- *"It's not who you are underneath, it's what you do that defines you."*
  (Rachel Dawes)

THE POST SHOW

Bible Passages

You may want to use these Bible passages during your movie discussion:

- Psalm 56:3-4

  "When I am afraid, I will trust in you. In God, whose word I praise, in God I trust; I will not be afraid. What can mortal man do to me?"

- Psalm 91:5

  "You will not fear the terror of night, nor the arrow that flies by day."

- Psalm 94:16

  "Who rise up for me against the wicked? Who will take a stand for me against evildoers?"

- Proverbs 31:8-9

  "Speak up for those who cannot speak for themselves, for the rights of all who are destitute. Speak up and judge fairly; defend the rights of the poor and needy."

- Isaiah 58:6

  "Is this not the kind of fasting I have chosen: to loose the chains of injustice and untie the cords of the yoke, to set the oppressed free and break every yoke?"

DISCUSSION

After the movie, use some or all of these questions to discuss the spiritual themes in *Batman Begins*.

 How did Bruce Wayne's fears affect his growth as a person?

 Do you think Christians should deal with their fears differently than those who don't believe in Jesus? Explain.

 Was Bruce justified in seeking vengeance? How did his obsession with vengeance hurt or help him? What do you think caused him to change his mind about seeking vengeance when he rebelled against Ducard?

 Do you ever find yourself in alignment with Ducard regarding your beliefs about justice? How far do you believe we should go in administering earthly punishment? Why?

 How did Bruce Wayne's efforts to bring justice to Gotham differ from the way of the League of Shadows? How would you compare this to a Christian vision of justice?

 Batman is portrayed as a rogue vigilante. Is there a danger in deciding upon what's just on our own? If so, what is the danger and how can we guard against it?

 In what way is Gotham a metaphor for society? In what way is Batman's guardianship over it a metaphor for our own lives?

 What do you find appealing about Bruce Wayne's life and his quest for justice as Batman? What do you find unappealing (what are the downsides)? How does that relate to your pursuit of justice in your own life?

PRAYER

Wrap things up by praying together. Have everyone take turns offering prayer requests. Remember to thank God for providing relief from our fears, and pray that he would guide us as we protect our own "Gothams."

THE END

THE MOVIE

STAR WARS

Genre: Science Fiction   **Length:** 123 minutes   **Rating:** PG

Quick Plot: In a galaxy far, far away, a humble farm boy is caught in a battle of good versus evil that affects the entire universe.

Why This Movie Is Great for Guys: Lasers, spaceships, adventure, and heroism! Luke's humble beginnings and heroic calling will encourage men to consider ways they've been called to a special destiny.

 Note: This movie is rated PG for sci-fi violence and brief mild language.

FOOD

Tasty Jawa Toes
Krayt Dragon Caviar
Alien Egg Salad Sandwiches
Chewy-bacca Brownies
Strawberry-Lemon Cantina Drinks

THE FOOD

Before your event, talk to the guys about dividing up the ingredients and supplies. Keep in mind that some items, such as dates and prosciutto, might cost a little more than others, and the Krayt Dragon Caviar requires more ingredients than the others. Maybe two people would like to share the cost of the Tasty Jawa Toes and the Krayt Dragon Caviar, while others each bring a couple of items.

What you'll need: Names:

Tasty Jawa Toes (serves 8)

24 pitted dates   _____

1 package thin-sliced prosciutto   _____

24 wooden toothpicks   _____

Strawberry-Lemon Cantina Drinks (serves 8)

1 can frozen lemonade concentrate   _____

1 container frozen sliced
strawberries, sweetened (thawed)   _____

**Chewy-bacca Brownies
(recipe on page 14)**   _____

**Krayt Dragon Caviar
(recipe on page 14)**   _____

**Alien Egg Salad Sandwiches
(recipe on page 15)**   _____

Easy Option Meal

If you'd rather avoid the kitchen, purchase egg salad, bread, and "frog-eye" salad at your local supermarket. Or, if you're feeling the desert planet vibe, pick up some southwestern food in the form of burritos and chips and salsa (opt for green chili for that otherworldly ambiance).

Don't forget about plates, napkins, and silverware. And if your "inner decorator" is clamoring to get out, *Star Wars* or space-themed party supplies are easy to find at most party or discount stores.

Tasty Jawa Toes

24 pitted dates
1 package of thin-sliced prosciutto
(a type of smoked ham, in the deli
aisle of your supermarket)

24 wooden toothpicks

Preheat your oven to 400 degrees. Cut the prosciutto slices into thirds, and wrap each piece around a date, securing it by sticking a toothpick through the middle. Place them on a baking sheet, and bake for 10 minutes or until the prosciutto becomes crispy on the edges, turning them with tongs halfway through. Allow to cool slightly, then place on a plate and serve. Serves 8.

Strawberry-Lemon Cantina Drinks

1 can frozen lemonade concentrate
1 container frozen sliced strawberries, sweetened (thawed)

Prepare the lemonade per the instructions on the can, and refrigerate. Thaw the berries in the fridge overnight. Before serving, add as many of the strawberries to the lemonade as you'd like (½ container is usually fine), and pour. Serves 8.

Chewy-bacca Brownies

1 package brownie mix
water, vegetable oil, and eggs called
    for on brownie box (usually ¼ cup
    water, ½ cup oil, and 2 eggs)

1 cup chocolate chips

Prepare the batter according to the directions on the box. Sprinkle the chocolate chips on the bottom of a greased 13x9-inch pan, and pour the batter over them. Bake for 28 minutes at 350 degrees, or until a toothpick inserted in the middle comes out clean. Remove from the oven, and allow to cool completely. For added fun, use yellow frosting to write "STAR WARS" in large marquee-style letters across the uncut brownies. Cover until ready to serve. Serves 10.

Krayt Dragon Caviar

1 package acini di pepe pasta (tiny
    round balls, found in your grocer's
    pasta aisle)
2 cups pineapple juice
2 eggs, beaten
1 cup sugar
2 tablespoons flour

½ teaspoon salt
2 cans crushed pineapple
1 container frozen whipped topping,
    thawed
½ cup shredded coconut
1½ cups mini marshmallows

Boil the pasta according to directions until it is al dente (softened but firm), then drain and rinse under cold running water. In a saucepan, combine the pineapple juice, eggs, sugar, flour, and salt, and boil until it thickens. Add the mixture to the pasta, along with the whipped topping and crushed pineapple. Cover and refrigerate overnight. Before serving, add the coconut and marshmallows. Mix and serve. Serves 10.

Alien Egg Salad Sandwiches

12 large eggs
½ cup mayonnaise
4 teaspoons Dijon-style mustard
4 tablespoons minced red onion

salt and pepper to taste
green food coloring
16 slices white bread

Put the eggs in a large saucepan or pot, and cover them with cold water. Bring the water to a boil, then cover and remove the pan from heat and let sit for 10 minutes. Next, fish the eggs out and put them in cold (ice) water. After 5 minutes, shell them and dice them into a large mixing bowl. Add a single small drop of green food coloring to the mayonnaise. Add the rest of the ingredients (except bread), and mix. Refrigerate until serving time. Spoon onto bread slices and cut the sandwiches crossway. Serves 8.

GETTING READY FOR THE SHOW

Making Dinner Happen

You have the home-court advantage here, so make it easy on yourself and have a cooking plan in mind before the event (decide how you'll assign tasks for meal prep). Then, when guests arrive, distribute photocopied recipes and have everyone work together to get the food on the table.

TalkStarters

Use these questions to prompt discussions as you eat together:
• How old were you when you first saw *Star Wars*? How many times have you seen it since? If you haven't seen it, where've you been?
• Who's your favorite *Star Wars* character? Why?
• Have you ever had a special mentor? Who was it, and what did that person teach you?
• Tell about a time you felt like your life was stuck at a dead end. What did you do about it?
• What special dreams of your future did you have when you were younger? How have they changed?

Star Wars Trivia Quiz

1. What year was *Star Wars* first released?
2. Which of the following actors were also considered for the role of Han Solo?
    A. James Caan
    B. Al Pacino
    C. Burt Reynolds
    D. Kurt Russell
3. Carrie Fisher, who played Princess Leia, is the daughter of which famous actress/dancer and actor/singer?

4. How tall is Peter Mayhew, who played Chewbacca the Wookiee?
5. Where did George Lucas get his inspiration for the character of Chewbacca?
6. George Lucas was responsible for the creation of which of these modern motion picture powerhouses?
    A. Industrial Light and Magic
    B. Pixar Animation Studios
    C. THX Sound
    D. Howard the Duck
7. Swordmaster Bob Anderson, who took on the role of Darth Vader during the key duel scenes in *Return of the Jedi* and *The Empire Strikes Back*, also played a key part in what other major motion picture trilogy?

Answers
1. 1977
2. All of them. Harrison Ford only read the part as a favor for the screen tests of the other characters, and surprisingly got the job.
3. Debbie Reynolds and Eddie Fisher
4. 7'3"
5. From seeing his Alaskan malamute dog, Indiana, sitting in the seat of his car.
6. All of them.
7. *The Lord of the Rings*, for which he was also swordmaster.

SHOWTIME!

The Pre-Show
Have everyone gather in the area where you'll show the movie. If you've just finished eating, you may want to provide a quick break for people to use the restroom. In preparation for your *Star Wars* viewing, why not engage in some *Star Wars* nerdliness? Have a friendly contest to see who can do the best *Star Wars* character impression (extra points for acting out the part).

THE SHOW

Genre: Science Fiction

Length: 123 minutes

Rating: PG for sci-fi violence and brief mild language (lasers and mild cursing)

Plot: Luke Skywalker is nothing but a farm boy on a backwater planet who yearns for escape and adventure. The opportunity is suddenly thrust upon him when his uncle buys a pair of robots who are carrying the secret plans for the Empire's new battle station.

Luke soon learns that this chance was no mere accident—whether he wants it or not, his life is about to change forever. Soon he finds himself racing across the galaxy with Obi-Wan Kenobi, one of the last Jedi Knights, and a smuggler crew, trying to evade the Empire and rescue a princess. They must deliver the plans that hold the only hope for defeating the Empire's planet-destroying superweapon, before the Empire can use *it* to destroy *them*!

THE POST SHOW

Bible Passages

You may want to use these Bible passages during your movie discussion:

- Jeremiah 1:5, 8

  " 'Before I formed you in the womb I knew you, before you were born I set you apart; I appointed you as a prophet to the nations…Do not be afraid of them, for I am with you and will rescue you,' declares the Lord."

- Ephesians 1:4a

  "For he chose us in him before the creation of the world to be holy and blameless in his sight."

- 1 Corinthians 2:13-14

  "This is what we speak, not in words taught us by human wisdom but in words taught by the Spirit, expressing spiritual truths in spiritual words. The man without the Spirit does not accept the things that come from the Spirit of God, for they are foolishness to him, and he cannot understand them, because they are spiritually discerned."

- John 16:5-8

  "Now I am going to him who sent me, yet none of you asks me, 'Where are you going?' Because I have said these things, you are filled with grief. But I tell you the truth: It is for your good that I am going away. Unless I go away, the Counselor will not come to you; but if I go, I will send him to you. When he comes, he will convict the world of guilt in regard to sin and righteousness and judgment."

DISCUSSION

After the movie, use some or all of these questions to discuss the spiritual themes in *Star Wars*.

 What similarities are there between the idea of the Force and the reality of God? What are the key differences?

Just for Fun!

Got a few extra minutes? Quiz everyone on the following *Star Wars* movie quotes.

WHO SAID:

- *"May the Force be with you."*
  (Obi-Wan Kenobi)

- *"Raaaarrrrrgghh!"*
  (Chewbacca)

- *"Help me, Obi-Wan Kenobi, you're my only hope."*
  (Princess Leia)

- *"You will never find a more wretched hive of scum and villainy."*
  (Obi-Wan Kenobi)

- *"Hokey religions and ancient weapons are no match for a good blaster at your side."*
  (Han Solo)

- *"When I left you I was but a learner, now I am the master."*
  (Darth Vader)

- *"I have a very bad feeling about this."*
  (Luke Skywalker)

- *"No reward is worth this."*
  (Han Solo)

- *"That's no moon. It's a space station."*
  (Obi-Wan Kenobi)

 How do you think Luke felt when he discovered that his father was a Jedi? How much does it matter who your parents are or were? Why?

 How did Obi-Wan's death change Luke's responsibilities? Why might it be necessary or helpful for us to lose our mentors?

 Why do you think the classic theme of the common boy who becomes a hero resonates so strongly with people? What events in the Bible tell a similar story, and what have these accounts meant to you?

 The change in Luke's home situation ultimately pushed him out of his comfort zone to follow Ben's calling. Tell about a time you experienced something like this.

 How is Luke's struggle to trust the Force similar to our struggle to trust the Holy Spirit? What makes it hard for you to trust God?

 Was Darth Vader right about the Force being more powerful than the Death Star? In what sense? How does that message apply to our own world?

 What about this story really appeals to you or excites you? What does this tell you about your personality and desires? How are those desires being met (or not) in your own life?

PRAYER

Close the evening with a prayer. Take time for prayer requests, and pray for everyone in the group. Remember to thank God for choosing us as his messengers and for his gift of the Holy Spirit. Especially remember to pray for renewed excitement for the great adventure we're part of with God as our Father.

MIRACLE

Genre: Drama   **Length:** 136 minutes   **Rating:** PG

Quick Plot: Considered by some to be the most emotional moment in sports history, a young, relatively inexperienced United States hockey team scores an unforgettable victory over the Soviet Union on the road to the Gold in the 1980 Olympics.

Why This Movie Is Great for Guys: This movie is better than watching Monday night football with your buddies! Added bonus: It's about the ultimate contest of athletic achievement—the Olympics. It doesn't matter how many replays we've seen of the final few minutes of that famous game with the Soviet Union—it still gives us goose bumps. *Miracle* will prompt discussions about teamwork, perseverance, faith, and the meaning of victory.

 Note: This movie is rated PG for language and some rough sports action.

FOOD

Hockey Dogs
Super Nachos
Drinks (soda, iced tea, water)
Goalie's Orange Slush
Microwave Popcorn

Before your event, talk to the guys about dividing up the ingredients and supplies. Keep in mind that some items may cost a bit more than others, so two people could share the cost of those items while others each bring a couple of other ingredients.

Easy Option Meal

If your group would rather stay "in the rink" than in the kitchen, imagine what vendors would serve at a hockey game and follow suit. Pick up nachos and hamburgers from local fast-food restaurants, and provide soda and popcorn.

Stadium snack bars provide napkins and plastic ware, so make sure those are available during your Dinner and a Movie event.

What you'll need: Names:

Hockey Dogs (serves 8)

1 package of 8 wieners   _____

1 package of 8 hot dog buns   _____

assorted condiments   _____

Super Nachos (serves 8)

1 pound ground beef   _____

16-ounce package processed cheese product   _____

10-ounce can diced tomatoes and green chilies   _____

1 jar salsa   _____

1 onion   _____

4 jalapeno peppers   _____

1 can diced olives   _____

2 bags tortilla chips   _____

1 bag microwave popcorn for every 2 people   _____

beverages (soda, iced tea)   _____

Goalie's Orange Slush (recipe on page 21)   _____

Hockey Dogs

1 package of 8 wieners
1 package of 8 hot dog buns

assorted condiments

It doesn't get easier than this! Either grill or boil the wieners, serve with buns, and offer an assortment of condiments such as ketchup, mustard, and relish—maybe even sauerkraut (just like a hockey stadium vendor). Serves 8.

Super Nachos

2 bags tortilla chips
1 pound ground beef
16-ounce package processed
  cheese product
10-ounce can diced tomatoes and
  green chilies

1 jar salsa
1 onion, diced
4 jalapeno peppers, diced
1 can olives, diced

Spread tortilla chips onto cookie sheet or shallow baking pan and place in 200-degree oven.

Over low to medium heat, brown the ground beef and season as desired.

Meanwhile, cut the cheese product into cubes. Combine with tomatoes and green chilies in microwave-safe bowl. Microwave for 2 minutes, stir, and microwave again for 2 more minutes. The cheese sauce should be smooth and creamy.

Remove chips from oven, and spread onto two large platters. Pour cheese sauce over chips, then spoon browned meat over cheese. Pour salsa over meat, and sprinkle remaining ingredients over all. Serve warm. Serves 8.

Making Dinner Happen

You have the home-court advantage here, so make it easy on yourself and have a cooking plan in mind before the event (decide how you'll assign tasks for meal prep). Then, when guests arrive, distribute photocopied recipes and have everyone work together to get the food on the table.

Goalie's Orange Slush

6-ounce can of frozen orange juice
1 cup milk
1 cup water

½ cup sugar
1 teaspoon vanilla
10-12 ice cubes

Shortly before guests arrive, mix ingredients in blender until smooth, then pour into individual glasses. Place glasses in freezer until movie starts. Serves 6.

GETTING READY FOR THE SHOW

TalkStarters

Use these questions to prompt discussions as you eat together:

• If the Winter Olympics were reduced to only one sport, which sport do you think should be the "survivor"? Which should be the first to go?

• Which do you find more exciting: summer or winter Olympics? Why?

• The average age on the "miracle" U.S. hockey team was 21 years old. What dreams and goals did you have when you were 21 years old? (Or, if you're not 21 yet, what dreams and goals do you have for when you reach 21?)

• Tell about a time you worked with a team to accomplish something seemingly impossible. What was the outcome? In what way were you impacted by the experience?

• Tell your favorite true story about someone winning against the odds.

Hockey Trivia Quiz

1. What year was the first hockey game played in North America?
2. What makes the Stanley Cup different from all other sports trophies?
3. Which hockey team has won the Stanley Cup the most?
4. In what year did goalies start wearing masks?
5. Which national teams did the United States hockey team play in the 1980 Olympics?
6. Since 1920, which two countries have won the most Olympic gold medals?
7. What year did NHL players start playing in the Olympics?

Answers
1. 1860 or 1875—the actual date is disputed.
2. First, it is the oldest trophy. Second, it has the names of the winning players, coaches, management, and club staff engraved on it. Third, each winning player and team management member gets to take the Cup home for a day to share with family and friends.
3. Montreal Canadiens
4. 1959
5. Sweden, Czechoslovakia, Norway, Romania, West Germany, Russia, Finland
6. Canada and Soviet Union
7. 1998

SHOWTIME!

The Pre-Show

Have everyone gather in the area where you'll show the movie. If you've just finished eating, you may want to provide a quick break for people to use the restroom.

THE SHOW

Genre: Drama

Length: 136 minutes

Rating: PG for language and some rough sports action

Plot: We already know how the story ends: The United States hockey team, an underdog squad coached by visionary Herb Brooks, turns the Olympic Games upside down with their victory over the Soviet Union in the medal round and then over Finland for the Gold in 1980.

But this movie is more than just a recap of sports history on the rink. It chronicles the journey of the team itself—beginning, in fact, before the team has actually materialized. Coach Brooks must first convince the United States Olympic Committee that his selection process is sound, even though it defies convention and the preferences of the committee's hockey members. And there is reason for the USOC to be concerned: The squad Brooks puts together is young, a bit unpolished, and some have grudges against each other based on old college rivalries. In a few words, things don't look so good.

Brooks knows what he's doing, though. Throughout grueling practices, drills, and even humiliating punishment for poor performance, the team begins to evolve into a formidable presence on the ice. And just as important, they learn—sometimes the hard way—principles of teamwork, leadership, and mutual respect.

The movie entertains and inspires with glimpses "behind the scenes" and with exciting game footage, but it's the climactic showdown at Lake Placid that leaves us almost slack-jawed with awe. No matter how many times we've seen replays of the United States' victory over the honed and skilled Soviet team, we can't help but join the crowd's frenzied elation during the game's final seconds.

The movie is aptly named.

THE POST SHOW

Bible Passages

You may want to use these Bible passages during your movie discussion:

• Mark 1:16-18

"As Jesus walked beside the Sea of Galilee, he saw Simon and his brother Andrew casting a net into the lake, for they were fishermen. 'Come, follow me,' Jesus said, 'and I will make you fishers of men.' At once they left their nets and followed him."

• Romans 8:37

"No, in all these things we are more than conquerors through him who loved us."

• Psalm 37:25

"I was young and now I am old, yet I have never seen the righteous forsaken, or their children begging bread."

• Ephesians 4:4

"There is one body and one Spirit—just as you were called to one hope when you were called."

• Psalm 104:1

"Praise the Lord, O my soul. O Lord my God, you are very great; you are clothed with splendor and majesty."

DISCUSSION

After the movie, use some or all of these questions to discuss the spiritual themes in *Miracle*.

 The U.S. hockey team assembled, practiced, and played for the goal of winning the Olympic Gold. Who's on your "life's team," and what parts do they play?

 Coach Brooks had preselected his preliminary roster for the American team, explaining: "I'm not looking for the best players, I'm looking for the right ones." What's the difference between the two? Do you agree with his selection method? Have you ever used similar criteria to choose between two options?

Tell about a time you had to work toward a common goal (at work, in ministry, or on a sports team, for instance) with someone you didn't really get along with. What happened?

 The U.S. hockey team had youthful energy, but the Soviet team had more experience. In terms of life in general, which attribute do you think is more valuable? Explain.

 The victory of the United States team seemed to give people a new hope for miracles and a belief in the "underdog." What gives people that hope and belief today?

 What "miracle" in your own life do you hope to experience?

 In a passionate speech to his team, Coach Brooks tells them that they were born to play hockey...that this was their time. Imagine a similar speech given to you: "You were born to be a Christian...this is your time." Time for what? What do you need to accomplish? How can Christians "win the Gold"?

PRAYER

End the evening by praying together. Ask for prayer requests. Encourage each person to share one specific way to put into practice the lessons learned from the movie *Miracle*. Have each person pray for someone else in the group; for example, everyone could pray for the person on his left.

THE END

RAIDERS OF THE LOST ARK

Genre: Action/Adventure   **Length:** 115 minutes   **Rating:** PG

Quick Plot: An American archaeologist in the 1930s goes on a dangerous adventure to find the long-lost ark of the covenant before the Nazis get their hands on it.

Why This Movie Is Great for Guys: What's not to like about a never-give-up hero who, instead of superpowers, uses nothing more than brains and grit (and his ever-handy bullwhip)? Guys will explore themes of heavenly power and earthly treasures.

 Note: This film is rated PG for intense action sequences, some gory violence (melting faces and such), and some brief language.

FOOD

Peruvian Jungle Skewers
Hidden Treasure Mashed Potatoes
Drinks (soda, iced tea, or ice water)
Berry & Brownie Skewers
Trail Mix With Poison-Free Dates

THE FOOD

Before your Dinner and a Movie event, talk to the guys about dividing up the ingredients and supplies. Keep in mind that some items, such as meat, cost more than others. Perhaps two people would like to share the cost of the meat, while others each bring a couple of items.

What you'll need: Names:

Peruvian Jungle Skewers

½ pound beef (cut into two-inch chunks) per person _____

3-4 papaya or mango chunks (2-inch) per person _____

½ bell pepper per person _____

½ small onion per person _____

salt and pepper _____

steak or barbecue sauce _____

wooden skewers, 2-3 per person _____

Hidden Treasure Mashed Potatoes (serves 8)

8 large russet potatoes _____

2 teaspoons salt _____

4 tablespoons butter _____

2 cups milk _____

1 package mixed chopped vegetables (frozen or fresh carrots, peas, and broccoli) _____

salt and pepper _____

Trail Mix With Poison-Free Dates

1 large package trail mix _____

1 package dried dates _____

Berry and Brownie Skewers (recipe on page 28) _____

beverages _____

Easy Option Meal

If you prefer quicker meal prep, buy a platter of chicken nuggets at your supermarket deli or chicken restaurant and skewer the nuggets along with canned pineapple chunks. You can also grab a bucket of pre-made mashed potatoes and a carton of veggies and mix them together. And if you don't feel like making fresh brownies, buy packages of brownie bites at your local grocer.

Pick up inexpensive, disposable wooden skewers at your supermarket, and don't forget napkins and dinnerware.

Peruvian Jungle Skewers

½ pound beef, cut into two-inch
  chunks, per person
3-4 two-inch chunks of papaya or
  mango per person

½ bell pepper per person
½ small onion per person
salt and pepper
wooden skewers

Soak wooden skewers in water for 15 minutes, then slide chunks of beef, papaya or mango, peppers, and onions onto skewers (about two skewers per person). Grill on medium-high heat until desired doneness. Serve with steak sauce and/or barbecue sauce.

Hidden Treasure Mashed Potatoes

8 large russet potatoes (peeled and
  rinsed)
2 teaspoons salt
4 tablespoons butter
2 cups milk, approximately

1 package mixed chopped
  vegetables (frozen or fresh
  carrots, peas, and broccoli)
salt and pepper

Quarter the peeled potatoes, and put in large pot with cold water and salt until just covered. Boil for 20 minutes or until fork-tender. Meanwhile, steam or boil vegetables until tender. Remove potatoes from heat, and beat in butter and milk to desired consistency. Salt and pepper to taste. Fold vegetables (the "hidden treasures") into mashed potatoes. Serves 8.

Trail Mix With Poison-Free Dates

1 large package of trail mix
1 package of dried dates

Combine trail mix with dates in a large bowl, and serve while watching the movie. Laugh at the traitorous monkey when he eats the poisonous date. Ensure your guests that the mix you've provided is free of such toxins. Serves 8.

Berry and Brownie Skewers

3-4 fresh strawberries per person
1 package of brownie mix

wooden skewers (1-2 per person)

Make brownies according to package directions. When cooled, cut into one-inch squares. Slide brownie bites onto skewers, alternating with strawberries. Serves 8.

Making Dinner Happen

You have the home-court advantage here, so make it easy on yourself and have a cooking plan in mind before the event (decide how you'll assign tasks for meal prep). Then, when guests arrive, distribute photocopied recipes and have everyone work together to get the food on the table.

GETTING READY FOR THE SHOW

TalkStarters

Use these questions to prompt discussions as you eat together:
- Think of historic artifacts such as Noah's ark, the Dead Sea Scrolls, remnants of chariots in the Red Sea, and others from biblical accounts. Which would you most like to discover—or touch, or see? Why?
- When you were a kid, what was the most valuable treasure you owned? How valuable is that treasure to you now?
- Why do you think people spend so much time "hunting" after earthly treasures?
- What's a quality you treasure in your friends, or hunt for when you're looking for a new friend?

Harrison Ford/Indiana Jones Trivia Quiz

1. What was Harrison Ford's profession when George Lucas tapped him to act in *American Graffiti*?
2. How many Academy Awards has Ford won?
3. Approximately how much money have all of Ford's movies totaled at the box office?
4. Who was originally cast in the role of *Indiana Jones*?
5. How many snakes were used in the production of *Raiders of the Lost Ark*?
6. How did George Lucas come up with the name "Indiana Jones"?
7. Who is your favorite Harrison Ford character from any movie? Why?

Answers
1. Carpenter
2. None
3. More than $3 billion
4. Tom Selleck
5. 7,000
6. Lucas' pet dog was named Indiana. Lucas called his main character Indiana Smith up until the first day of movie production, when director Steven Spielberg changed it to Jones.

SHOWTIME!

The Pre-Show

Have everyone gather in the area where you'll show the movie. If you've just finished eating, you may want to provide a quick break for people to use the restroom.

When everyone has gathered, serve the Berry and Brownie Skewers along with Trail Mix With Poison-Free Dates to anyone who's ready for dessert or snacks.

THE SHOW

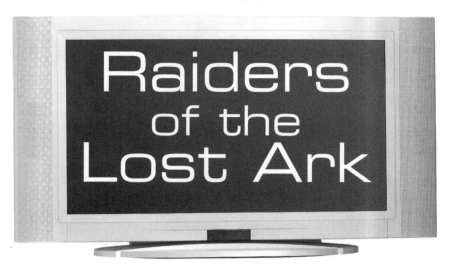

Raiders
of the
Lost Ark

Genre: Action/Adventure

Length: 115 minutes

Rating: PG for intense action sequences, some gory violence, and some brief language

Plot: The U.S. government has learned that the Nazis are searching for the ancient ark of the covenant, and they want renowned archaeologist Indiana Jones to find it first. So Jones grabs his revolver, his whip, and his well-worn leather hat and heads off to Nepal to meet with his former colleague, Abner Ravenwood, who holds a clue that will lead him to the location of the ark.

Alas, once in Nepal Jones discovers that Ravenwood has died, but not before giving his daughter, Marion, the relic Indiana Jones is looking for. Here's where things begin to get complicated: Marion happens to be a former girlfriend of Jones. But Nazi agent Toht burns down Marion's bar in an attempt to steal the relic, and she and Indy flee to Cairo.

While in Egypt, Jones realizes that the Nazis, led by his longtime nemesis Dr. Rene Belloq, are already digging for the ark. But Jones' old friend Sallah helps him locate the actual location, where they find the ark in its hidden tomb. Alas, again. Because this is an action movie with nonstop thrills and obstacles, Belloq and the Nazis always seem to be a step ahead of Jones. They steal the ark, leaving him and Marion to die underground.

All seems lost. There's no way out. Escape is impossible. But wait… Indiana Jones stars in another movie after this one, so don't move from the edge of your seat. Indy isn't finished yet!

THE POST SHOW

Bible Passages

You may want to use these Bible passages during your movie discussion:

- Exodus 25:10-22
  This Scripture passage describes the construction of the ark of the covenant and its purpose for the people of Israel.

- Matthew 6:19-21
  "Do not store up for yourselves treasures on earth, where moth and rust destroy, and where thieves break in and steal. But store up for yourselves treasures in heaven, where moth and rust do not destroy, and where thieves do not break in and steal. For where your treasure is, there your heart will be also."

- Isaiah 10:15
  "Does the ax raise itself above him who swings it, or the saw boast against him who uses it? As if a rod were to wield him who lifts it up, or a club brandish him who is not wood!"

- Isaiah 45:11-12
  "This is what the Lord says—the Holy One of Israel, and its Maker: Concerning things to come, do you question me about my children, or give me orders about the work of my hands? It is I who made the earth and created mankind upon it. My own hands stretched out the heavens; I marshaled their starry hosts."

- Ephesians 1:18-21
  "I pray also that the eyes of your heart may be enlightened in order that you may know the hope to which he has called you, the riches of his glorious inheritance in the saints, and his incomparably great power for us who believe. That power is like the working of his mighty strength, which he exerted in Christ when he raised him from the dead and seated him at his right hand in the heavenly realms, far above all rule and authority, power and dominion, and every title that can be given, not only in the present age but also in the one to come."

Just for Fun!

Got a few extra minutes? Quiz everyone on the following *Raiders of the Lost Ark* movie quotes.

WHO SAID:
- *"Snakes. Why did it have to be snakes?"*
  (Indiana Jones)

- *"I don't believe in magic. A lot of superstitious hocus-pocus."*
  (Indiana Jones)

- *"I don't know. I'm making this up as I go."*
  (Indiana Jones)

- *"We are merely passing through history. [The ark] is history."*
  (Dr. Rene Belloq)

- *"You can't do this to me. I'm an American!"*
  (Marion Ravenwood)

- *"It's not the years, honey. It's the mileage."*
  (Indiana Jones)

- *"You Americans, you're all the same. Always overdressing for the wrong occasions."*
  (Arnold Toht)

- *"You want to talk to God? Let's go see him together. I've got nothing better to do."*
  (Indiana Jones)

DISCUSSION

After the movie, use some or all of these questions to discuss the spiritual themes in *Raiders of the Lost Ark.*

 Why do you think this is one of the most popular adventure films of all time?

 How do you think Indy's opinion about supernatural power changed during the course of the story? What do you think caused that change in perspective?

 At one point Indy says, "I'm making this up as I go." Do you ever feel like that in your faith journey? Why or why not?

 How were Indy's and Belloq's motives for pursuing the treasure the same? How were they different?

 Belloq believed the ark was "a transmitter...for speaking to God." Do you think he was right or wrong about that? Explain.

 The Nazis in the movie believed the ark would make their army invincible, just as it made armies in the Old Testament invincible. Do you think this would have worked for the Nazis in real life? Why or why not?

 Do you think we have the ability to tap into God's power? Explain your thoughts.

 In what ways would you like to see God's power in your life?

 What faith connections can you make between "seeking heavenly treasures" and "using God's power"?

 Why do you think the U.S. government stored the ark away in the vast warehouse at the end of the movie? What would you have done with it?

PRAYER

End your group's time together in prayer. Have each person share one earthly treasure he is thankful for and one heavenly treasure he'll commit to pursing in the coming week. Take turns praying aloud, thanking God for the temporary treasures he's given you, and asking for his wisdom and power as you pursue eternal treasures.

THE END

THE INCREDIBLES

Genre: Animated Adventure   **Length:** 115 minutes   **Rating:** PG

Quick Plot: Because Mr. Incredible is unable to give up his superhero life, he unwittingly draws his ex-superhero wife and superpower-gifted children into an adventure…one that may cost their lives.

Why This Movie Is Great for Guys: Superpowers! As Mr. Incredible comes to grips with his life, he must consider forfeiting the work and accomplishments that define who he is. He's also forced to consider his priorities—and how they impact his family. In a few words: We guys can identify with this one.

 Note: This animated movie might be fun for a father-son gathering. It is rated PG for action violence.

FOOD

Spamabob Appetizers
Roast Pork
Drinks (tropical punch, iced tea, ice water)
Tropical Hideout Fruit Plate

THE FOOD

When you're meeting super-villains at their exotic tropical island hideaways, you don't want to be poking at your plate asking, "What's *this* stuff?"

So, in consideration of your guests, refrain from serving anything poisonous, or that harbors harmful pieces of a hero's home planet, or that stains a super suit.

Enhance and enliven your menu by stringing pool lights around the dining area, planting a few tiki torches by the front door, or hanging a stuffed parrot someplace prominent. Suggest that guys wear shorts and Hawaiian shirts.

And given that tropical food can get expensive, have guests contribute by bringing specific dinner ingredients.

Easy Option Meal

If you'd rather just reheat than cook from scratch, notify guys that, in the same way the Parr family has a "leftover" night, so will you. Tell men to clean out their refrigerators and bring what they find—as long as the food is still edible. Anything green should be green on *purpose*.

Don't forget the napkins and beverages. Tropical punch works well here, especially if you drop by a party store and buy little umbrellas. And remember the silverware: You're super*heroes*, not super*slobs*.

What you'll need: Names:

Spamabob Appetizers (serves 8)

skewers   _____

2 cans Spam   _____

3 green peppers   _____

2 red onions   _____

Tropical Hideout Fruit Plate (serves 8)

2 cans pineapple chunks   _____

3 papayas, sliced   _____

1-2 bunches grapes   _____

1 coconut (whole)   _____

5-6 bananas   _____

beverages (fruit punch)   _____

Roast Pork (recipe on page 35)   _____

Spamabob Appetizers

No kidding: Spam is *enormously* popular in Hawaii. Assuming your super-villain's taste reflects local sensibilities, and his hideout is in Hawaii, no meal is complete without spiced ham.

2 cans Spam (cut into one-inch squares and fried)

3 green peppers, chopped into bite-sized chunks

2 red onions, chopped into bite-sized chunks

8 skewers

Using a grill, create shish kebobs featuring Spam. Use your favorite grilling technique; we wouldn't *think* of telling you how to use your grill...Serves 8.

Tropical Hideout Fruit Plate

Serve in a bowl, but don't prepare before guests arrive lest the banana chunks look less than appealing.

2 cans pineapple chunks

3 papayas, sliced

1-2 bunches grapes

1 coconut, meat chopped into chunks

5-6 bananas, cut into chunks

Be generous in your portions; this fruit plate will double as your munchies during the show. Assuming your guys will eat healthy, one medium platter per eight guys should do the trick.

Making Dinner Happen

You have the home-court advantage here, so make it easy on yourself and have a cooking plan in mind before the event (decide how you'll assign tasks for meal prep). Then, when guests arrive, distribute photocopied recipes and have everyone work together to get the food on the table.

Roast Pig

Pork is a traditional luau party food, but rather than roast an entire pig, take the easy route: Cook a pork roast. Here's a recipe that approximates that authentic luau taste...

5-pound pork butt
Liquid Smoke
salt

Preheat oven to 325 degrees. Score the fat of the port butt into 1-inch squares and rub salt into the fat. Sprinkle Liquid Smoke over the meat and fat. Wrap meat in aluminum foil, and bake for 4-5 hours. Shred meat, and serve in sandwiches. Serves 10-15.

GETTING READY FOR THE SHOW

TalkStarters

Use these questions to prompt discussions as you eat together:
• When you were young, who was your favorite superhero?
• If you were a superhero facing retirement, what would you do as a second career? Why?
• What's something you could once do with ease that you can no longer do? How does it feel to no longer have that ability or option?
• What were your "glory days"? (Or, do you think they're still to come?) Do you have a desire to relive that time? Why or why not?
• Would you say your best days are ahead of you...or behind you? Why?

Superhero Trivia Quiz

1. What year was the first Superman comic book released?
2. Which actress stars in two separate comic book movies (about two different superheroes)?
3. What's the first—and last—name of Batman's butler?
4. The Human Torch is part of which group of superheroes?
5. What is the Hulk's other name?
6. Red Skull is the archenemy of which superhero?
7. Who played the Hulk in the television series *The Incredible Hulk?* For extra points, who played his alter ego?

Answers
1. 1938
2. Halle Berry—she's portrayed both Storm (X-Men) and Catwoman.
3. Alfred Pennyworth
4. Fantastic Four
5. Dr. Bruce Banner
6. Captain America
7. Lou Ferrigno, Bill Bixby

SHOWTIME!

The Pre-Show

Have everyone gather in the area where you'll show the movie. If you've just finished eating, you may want to provide a quick break for people to use the restroom.

When everyone has gathered, pass around the fruit plate so guys can have some munchies while viewing the movie.

THE SHOW

Genre: Animated Adventure

Length: 115 minutes

Rating: PG for action violence

Plot: Once America's favorite superhero, Mr. Incredible finds that his crime-fighting career evaporates when a spate of lawsuits drives superheroes into hiding—including him and his wife, Elastigirl.

Retiring to the suburbs under the name Bob Parr, Mr. Incredible settles into his life as a family man with three children. These aren't ordinary kids, mind you—like their parents, the oldest two have superpowers, while the baby's super-abilities are, as yet, untested. But our superhero spends the next 15 years in boring, routine jobs... until a mysterious message gives him the chance to once again pull on the super suit for an adventure.

Bob risks everything to relive a bit of the old glory—compromising his cover as just another cog in an insurance company, he uses his superpowers once again. But as he launches into his revitalized career with enthusiasm, he unwittingly drags his family into unexpected dangers that force them to unleash the superpowers they'd been forbidden to use.

They say the family that plays together stays together, and the same can be said for the family that combats super-villians on uncharted tropical islands. Each weighing in with their specialized powers, the Incredibles join forces to fend off a hostile Omnidroid 9000 and the evil Syndrome (you'll have to watch the movie to find out what those are).

Bible Passages

You may want to use these Bible passages during your movie discussion:

- **1 Corinthians 1:30-31**
  "It is because of him that you are in Christ Jesus, who has become for us wisdom from God—that is, our righteousness, holiness and redemption. Therefore, as it is written: 'Let him who boasts boast in the Lord.' "

- **Philippians 3:8**
  "What is more, I consider everything a loss compared to the surpassing greatness of knowing Christ Jesus my Lord, for whose sake I have lost all things. I consider them rubbish, that I may gain Christ."

- **Psalm 29:3-4**
  "The voice of the Lord is over the waters; the God of glory thunders, the Lord thunders over the mighty waters. The voice of the Lord is powerful; the voice of the Lord is majestic."

- **Proverbs 3:5-6**
  "Trust in the Lord with all your heart and lean not on your own understanding; in all your ways acknowledge him, and he will make your paths straight."

Just for Fun!

Got a few extra minutes? Quiz everyone on the following *Incredibles* movie quotes.

WHO SAID:

- *"No matter how many times you save the world, it always manages to get back in jeopardy again. Sometimes I just want it to stay saved!"*
  (Mr. Incredible)

- *"You always, always say 'Be true to yourself,' but you never say which part of yourself to be true to! Well, I finally figured out who I am: I am your ward. IncrediBoy!"*
  (Buddy Pine)

- *"Oh, ho ho! You sly dog! You got me monologuing! I can't believe it."*
  (Buddy Pine)

- *"We're dead! We're dead! We survived, but we're dead!"*
  (Dashiell "Dash" Parr)

- *"Well, with counseling, I think you'll come to forgive me."*
  (Mr. Incredible)

DISCUSSION

After the movie, use some or all of these questions to discuss the spiritual themes in *The Incredibles*.

 Which character in this movie did you especially relate to? Why?

 We don't need to be psychologists to see that Mr. Incredible was, at one time in the movie, depressed. What do you think about the way he dealt with his depression?

 What changes did you see in Mr. Incredible throughout the movie? Would you mind seeing any of those changes in your own life? Explain.

Mr. Incredible is obviously a proud guy. Of what is he proud? What pride issues do you think men typically deal with in life?

As Christians, we're sometimes taught that pride is wrong. Do you agree? disagree? Why?

Envision Mr. Incredible's trophy room at home. If you had a trophy room, what sort of trophies would you most like to have on the shelves and walls? Are you working to achieve any of these "trophies"? If so, how?

What can this movie teach Christian guys about priorities?

...about communication with others?

...about family?

In the last few frames of the movie, the Parr family dons their masks. What message do you think this is supposed to convey?

PRAYER

End the evening by praying together. Ask for prayer requests. Encourage each man to share one specific way he can put into practice a lesson learned from *The Incredibles*. Ask each man to pray for someone else in the group, perhaps by pairing up and praying for partners.

THE MOVIE
SIGNS

Genre: Drama/Mystery   **Length:** 106 minutes   **Rating:** PG-13

Quick Plot: While space aliens begin taking over the earth, a disenchanted reverend struggles with his anger and doubt regarding God.

Why This Movie Is Great for Guys: It's suspenseful; it's packed with intergalactic intrigue… what more could guys want? Ah—there is more: The movie poses thought-provoking questions about faith, family, and the connectedness of the world.

 Note: This movie is rated PG-13 for frightening moments.

FOOD

Like-Mama-Made-When-She-Was-Busy Corn Pudding
Corn Tortilla Tacos (à la Alien)
Drinks (soda, iced tea, ice water)
Popcorn munchies

THE FOOD

It doesn't take long before we see that the aliens in *Signs* have an affinity for corn. Their crop circles never appear in fields of green beans, pastures of parsley, or in hillsides of hay. Nope—it's always corn. So serve your guests what is clearly a space-explorer's delicacy: corn. If it's in season, include corn on the cob, but just in case, we've offered other ways to provide every alien's dream: an all-corn repast. Before your Dinner and a Movie event, talk to the guys about contributing ingredients to spread out the cost a bit.

Easy Option Meal

Want to avoid the kitchen? Granted, it's a departure from the corn-y menu, but try this: In the movie, Reverend Hess' family meets at a pizzeria for a quick bite to eat. You'll do the same—except for the pizzeria part. Order delivery, and do a bit of manly bonding by having your guests wear hats made of tin foil when the delivery person arrives. Act natural. Tip liberally.

What you'll need: Names:

Corn Tortilla Tacos (à la Alien)

2 corn tortillas per person   _____

¼ pound ground round per person   _____

refried beans   _____

shredded cheese   _____

canned sliced olives   _____

chopped tomatoes   _____

lettuce   _____

salsa (a variety of flavors)   _____

beverages (soda, iced tea, water) _____

microwave popcorn   _____

Like-Mama-Made-When-She-Was-Busy Corn Pudding (recipe on page 42)   _____

One more thing: Remember the napkins and beverages.

Corn Tortilla Tacos
(à la Alien)

2 corn tortillas per person
¼ pound seasoned ground round
  per person
refried beans
shredded cheese (we suggest sharp
  cheddar; the debate rages)

canned sliced olives
chopped tomatoes
shredded lettuce
salsa (mild...hot...incendiary; provide
  options)

One man's favorite taco is another man's *least* favorite taco, so place ingredients in separate dishes so guys can build their own tacos. It's hard to predict who'll like what, so be generous in provisions. Tip: A quarter pound of ground round is sufficient for about two tacos.

Like-Mama-Made-
When-She-Was-Busy Corn Pudding

8½-ounce box of instant corn muffin
  mix
16-ounce can of whole kernel corn—
  with juice
16-ounce can of creamed corn

1 stick of melted butter or
  margarine
1 cup sour cream
2 eggs

Mix all the ingredients until they're well blended, then pour the entire mess into a large, flat baking dish. Bake uncovered at 350 degrees for 45 to 50 minutes or until lightly browned.

Microwave or heat in oven when guests arrive. Serves 6-8.

Popcorn

bags of microwave popcorn
microwave
patience

If you like, you can provide seasonings for the popcorn such as Parmesan cheese, butter, colored sugar sprinkles, or other flavorings.

Making Dinner Happen

You have the home-court advantage here, so make it easy on yourself and have a cooking plan in mind before the event (decide how you'll assign tasks for meal prep). Then, when guests arrive, distribute photocopied recipes and have everyone work together to get the food on the table.

GETTING READY FOR THE SHOW

TalkStarters
Use these questions to prompt discussions as you eat together:
• What's your favorite song from high school days that you're now ashamed to admit you loved?
• What's a food you once enjoyed that now you never want to see or taste again?
• Think about who you were in high school. What's the most important change that has taken place in your life since then? Explain the significance of this change.

Signs Trivia Quiz (All Mel, All the Time):
1. What year was Gibson born?
2. What is Gibson's religious faith?
3. What actress received a gift-wrapped rat as a gift from Gibson?
4. In a production of "Romeo and Juliet" Gibson portrayed what character?
5. What is Gibson's full name?
6. What financial record did Gibson set in Australia?
7. For extra credit: Name three of Gibson's seven children.

Answers:
1. 1956 (January 3)
2. Roman Catholic. He has his own private church.
3. Julia Roberts—and he apparently never gave a reason.
4. Juliet. Note: It was an all-male production.
5. Mel's full name is Mel Columcille Gerard Gibson.
6. He was the first Australian actor to be paid a million dollars for a film role.
7. Hannah, Edward, Christian, Willie, Louis, Milo, and Tommy

SHOWTIME!

The Pre-Show
Have everyone gather in the area where you'll show the movie. If you've just finished eating, provide a quick break for people to use the restroom.

And serve popcorn. Any aliens in your midst will appreciate the gesture.

Signs

Genre: Drama/Mystery

Length: 106 minutes

Rating: PG-13 for frightening moments

Plot: Graham Hess, a former priest whose faith in God is severely tested by the untimely death of his wife, is left to raise their two young children on his Pennsylvania farm along with his simple-witted brother. Life presents normal challenges for the family, complicated only slightly by the son's asthma, but normalcy is shaken when unexplainable crop circles appear in the cornfield. First thought a hoax, the enigma continues to develop and Graham discovers that similar circles are appearing in fields across the globe.

Graham's farm—and family—continue to be targeted by the unknown beings responsible for the circles. The nerve-racking mystery begins to take its toll on the children, and his son buys a book about aliens in hopes of learning enough to outsmart them. In fact, after his first confrontation with one of the aliens, Graham comes home to find his family sitting on the sofa, wearing hats crafted from aluminum foil to deflect the extraterrestrials' ability to read their minds.

Graham has had enough: When the news reveals that UFOs have been sighted in over 270 cities and that the number is quickly growing, he takes aggressive measures to save his own family. Events spiral into a devastating showdown between outer-space aliens and humans, and the remainder of the movie is a nail-biting ride as the sadistic corpse-like aliens try to gain a foothold into his farmhouse—and access to his children.

The most memorable scenes are those where the weak show strength, and the doubtful gain redemption. This story considers what's behind life's circumstances: Is it coincidence or a higher power weaving a tapestry of purpose? Also considered: the nature of doubt, coping with loss, and forgiving others—as well as oneself.

THE POST SHOW

Bible Passages

You may want to use these Bible passages during your movie discussion:

- Psalm 57:2

  "I cry out to God Most High, to God, who fulfills his purpose for me."

- Matthew 14:31

  "Immediately Jesus reached out his hand and caught him. 'You of little faith,' he said, 'why did you doubt?' "

- Proverbs 1:33

  "But whoever listens to me will live in safety and be at ease, without fear of harm."

- Psalm 27:1

  "The Lord is my light and my salvation—whom shall I fear? The Lord is the stronghold of my life—of whom shall I be afraid?"

Just for Fun!

Got a few extra minutes? Quiz everyone on Mel Gibson movie quotes. In what movie did his character say:

- *"Love gives you wings. It makes you fly. I don't even call it love. I call it Geronimo. When you're in love, you'll jump right from the top of the Empire State and you won't care, screaming 'Geronimo' the whole way down."*
  (Conspiracy Theory)

- *"It's all for nothing if you don't have freedom."*
  (Braveheart)

- *"I don't make things difficult. That's the way they get all by themselves."*
  (Lethal Weapon)

- *"Every man dies—not every man really lives."*
  (Braveheart)

- *"Flied lice?"*
  (Lethal Weapon 4)

- *"I would rather die tomorrow than live a hundred years without knowing you."*
  (Pocahontas)

DISCUSSION

After the movie, use some or all of these questions to discuss the spiritual themes in *Signs*.

 Graham separates people into two groups: 1) people who see miracles and who feel as though someone is always with them, and 2) people who see the results of luck and who feel alone. Which group are you in? Why?

 How hard would it be to forgive someone whose thoughtlessness caused pain to you? to your wife or child?

 Do you believe anything is coincidental? How far does God's power reach into our everyday lives?

 The death of Graham's wife tested his faith beyond what he believed were its limits. Can real faith be broken by one life event? Explain your opinion.

 What were your feelings during the basement scene when Graham tells God, "Don't do this to me again...I hate you"? Can you relate to this scene? Why or why not?

 Graham's wife's last words ring strongly in the climax of the movie. Do you believe that God uses mysterious things like that to help us? Why or why not?

 What drew Graham back to his faith in God? Have you ever had a situation draw you back to God or into a deeper relationship with him? If so, share about that.

PRAYER

End the evening praying together. Ask men to form pairs and to pray for each other to understand God's power and see him working in their lives.

THE MOVIE
GALAXY QUEST

Genre: Adventure/Comedy   **Length:** 102 minutes   **Rating:** PG

Quick Plot: The sci-fi cast of a "Galaxy Quest" TV series must pull through when they're forced to not just play heroic space explorers…but to deliver the goods.

Why This Movie Is Great for Guys: In addition to spoofing Star Trek conventions, this movie delivers action, adventure, and comedy…plus the chance to ponder friendship, egotism, and the nature of faith.

 Note: This movie is rated PG for some action violence, mild language, and mild sensuality.

FOOD

English Breakfast:
Eggs
Ham
Tomatoes
Beans on Toast
Drinks (tea, orange juice, water)
Movie Snacks:
Gummy worms
Peanuts

Why Breakfast?

When dinner's served on the NSEA Protector, honored guests are offered regional cuisine from where they were raised. Captain Taggart is pleased—he gets a steak. Dr. Lazarus is less thrilled: Mistaking the actor for his character, his hosts serve the good doctor Kep-mok blood ticks. Live Kep-mok blood ticks. Clearly, the actor—a perpetually cranky British thespian—would have preferred something from London, not Kep-mok.

Right that wrong by providing your guests the meal Dr. Lazarus wishes he would have found on the table: a traditional English breakfast.

Add to the fun by speaking in your best English accent and calling everyone "Guv." This will actually be fun only for you, but since you're cooking, nobody will complain much.

Easy Option Meal

Since honored guests aboard the NSEA Protector were given food from their own regions, you could do the same. What's a local favorite where you live?

Whatever it is, serve it—as simply as possible.

And if all else fails, *everywhere* claims cooked chicken as its own. A bucket from the local outlet will do the trick.

Before your Dinner and a Movie event, talk to the guys and divide up the ingredients so that each contributes by bringing a couple of items.

What you'll need:	Names:
English Breakfast	
tomatoes (½ tomato per guy)	_____
eggs (2 per guy)	_____
ham (hefty, thick slice per guy)	_____
white bread (1 slice per guy)	_____
canned baked beans (two 28-ounce cans per 10 guys)	_____
gummy worms (13-ounce bag per 10 guys)	_____
dry-roasted peanuts (24-ounce jar per 10 guys)	_____
beverages (tea, orange juice, water)	_____

The traditional "full English breakfast" includes the following: fried or poached eggs, fried tomatoes, ham, and beans on toast (really). Here's how to make it happen...

Preheat your oven grill to medium.

Slice tomatoes in half—crosswise. Grill the ham, flipping slices often, removing and setting aside when brown. Add tomatoes to the grill and lightly grill, turning often. Set aside.

Open a can of baked beans and heat in a saucepan or a microwave until heated thoroughly.

Toast a piece of white bread for each guest.

Fry—over medium—two eggs for each guest.

For each guest, place two eggs, half tomato, ham, and a piece of toast on a plate. Plop a generous amount of baked beans on the piece of toast.

Assuming some items have grown cold (*real* cooks plan meals so each element is ready simultaneously—you are likely not a real cook), microwave each plate for 10 seconds.

Serve.

Notes for the Especially Culinarily Challenged:

To fry an egg, do the following:
Heat ½ teaspoon olive oil in a (trust us on this) nonstick pan. When oil is hot, break an egg into the pan and sprinkle a pinch of salt and half-pinch of pepper on the egg. Cover the pan and don't peek for 60 seconds. Steam released by the egg will cover the top of the egg. Maybe. Experiment with your stove setting and equipment *before* guests arrive.

To cut ham for an English breakfast:
Use fairly thick slices—man-size, not wimpy, pre-sliced deli cuts.

To open a can of beans:
If you don't know how to do *this*, abandon the breakfast and head for the nearest fried chicken takeout restaurant.

Remember napkins and beverages. Brew a kettle of English tea, but expect men to prefer more traditional beverages: coffee, orange juice, or water (no ice! This is a British breakfast!).

Making Dinner Happen

You have the home-court advantage here, so make it easy on yourself and have a cooking plan in mind before the event (decide how you'll assign tasks for meal prep). Then, when guests arrive, distribute photocopied recipes and have everyone work together to get the food on the table.

GETTING READY FOR THE SHOW

TalkStarters

Use these questions to prompt discussions as you eat together:

• Do you consider yourself to be a "geek" of any kind (like a comic book geek, a computer geek, or a *Star Trek* geek)? If so, do you wear this badge proudly?

• Imagine that you were voted "most likely to..." when in high school or grade school. What would the award have mentioned...and has it actually happened in your life?

• What life event or events have brought about the most transformation in your life? Explain.

• What transformation would you like to see in your life within the next 10 years?

Galaxy Quest Trivia Quiz

1. Why did the director of *Galaxy Quest* choose the name "Sarris" for his evil warlord?

2. Sigourney Weaver has appeared in other films featuring space creatures. What are two of those films?

3. Tim Allen went to prison for what crime?

4. *Galaxy Quest* is a parody of what science fiction television show?

5. For Trekkie Points: What was the mission of the USS Enterprise?

6. Trekkie Bonus Points: What is the meaning of Lieutenant Uhura's name?

7. Uber-Trekkie Bonus Points: How many years separated the cancellation of *Star Trek* and the first airing of *Star Trek: The Next Generation*?

Answers

1. Film critic Andrew Sarris once trashed director Mark Johnson's film *The Natural*. Apparently, this is payback of the sweetest kind.
2. *Alien* (1979), *Aliens* (1986), *Alien3* (1992), *Alien: Resurrection* (1997)
3. When Allen was 25, he served a 14-month prison term for possession of cocaine.
4. *Star Trek*
5. "To seek out new life and new civilizations, to boldly go where no man has gone before."
6. "Freedom"—in Swahili
7. 18 years

SHOWTIME!

The Pre-Show

Have everyone gather in the area where you'll show the movie. If you've just finished eating, you may want to provide a quick break for people to use the restroom.

Serve munchies. Since Kep-mok blood ticks are hard to find locally, substitute with bowls of gummy worms and dry roasted peanuts.

THE SHOW

Genre: Adventure/Comedy

Length: 102 minutes

Rating: PG

Plot: Years after their show was cancelled, the cast of *Galaxy Quest* is still pulling on the old costumes to appear at conventions and to make commercials. These publicity obligations are torturous and degrading for most of the cast—but not for Jason Nesmith, commander of TV series' NSEA *Protector*. He relishes whatever attention he can get.

And the attention is dwindling—on earth. The galactic fan base, on the other hand, is apparently just gaining momentum. Approached at a convention by what he assumes is a group of fans dressed as aliens, Jason agrees to accompany them to their amateur spaceship set. He's impressed and flattered by the authenticity of the *Protector* replica and attempts to humor his fans by stepping into his age-old role as Captain, but he quickly learns that these aliens are the real deal. In fact, they are Thermians, a peaceful race that had received 20-year-old transmissions of the *Galaxy Quest* TV series and considered the fictitious episodes to be true, historical documents. The spaceship he's been escorted to is not an amateur set—it's an exact replica of the series' *Protector*.

Before you can say *egomaniacal*, Jason assumes the lead in a real-life episode of space battle with an evil alien warlord. Summoning his earthly *Galaxy Quest* crew for help, the washed-up cast must prove their mettle in a galactic genocidal war threatening their new Thermian friends. But things rapidly turn from bad to worse when the Thermians discover that neither commander Jason Nesmith, nor his crew, are who they postured themselves to be.

Themes of ego, acceptance, and transformation are explored in this tale of heroism and…weirdness.

THE POST SHOW

Bible Passages

You may want to use these Bible passages during your movie discussion:

Just for Fun!

Got a few extra minutes? Quiz everyone on the following *Galaxy Quest* movie quotes.

WHO SAID:
- *"Never give up. Never surrender."*
  (Captain Taggart)

- *"By Grabthar's hammer, by the sons of Worvan, you shall be avenged."*
  (Dr. Lazarus)

- *"I remember that sound. That's a bad sound."*
  (Lt. Madison)

- *"It doesn't take a great actor to recognize a bad one."*
  (Captain Taggart)

- *"You know, what I could really use here is a cup holder and a couple of Advil."*
  (Captain Taggart)

- *"Hey guys, I just wanted you to know that the reactors won't take it; the ship is breaking apart and all that... Just FYI."*
  (Tech Sergeant Chen)

- Romans 12:1-2

  "And so, dear brothers and sisters, I plead with you to give your bodies to God because of all he has done for you. Let them be a living and holy sacrifice—the kind he will find acceptable. This is truly the way to worship him. Don't copy the behavior and customs of this world, but let God transform you into a new person by changing the way you think. Then you will learn to know God's will for you, which is good and pleasing and perfect." [NLT]

- Romans 12:3

  "For by the grace given me I say to every one of you: Do not think of yourself more highly than you ought, but rather think of yourself with sober judgment, in accordance with the measure of faith God has given you."

- Colossians 3:12

  "Therefore, as God's chosen people, holy and dearly loved, clothe yourselves with compassion, kindness, humility, gentleness and patience."

- 1 Samuel 2:3

  "Do not keep talking so proudly or let your mouth speak such arrogance, for the Lord is a God who knows, and by him deeds are weighed."

DISCUSSION

After the movie, use some or all of these questions to discuss the spiritual themes in *Galaxy Quest*.

 With which character in this movie did you most identify? Why?

 Some characters in this movie went through a significant transformation. Whose did you notice—and what was the transformation?

How do you think the crew of actors will relate to each other in the future? Why?

 The actor playing Dr. Lazarus was dismayed about being typecast. In what ways have you been "typecast" in life? What might it take to break out of that mold?

 What trait do you think is most important for a leader to have? Who do you know who best exemplifies that trait?

 For a few of the characters, faith in what seems impossible is required for the battle to be won. When have you had to rely on faith in something that seemed beyond belief? What happened?

 How might this movie support or challenge the notion that "you are what you believe you are"?

 What can this movie teach Christian guys about friendship?

...teamwork?

...transformation?

PRAYER

End the evening by praying together. Ask men to share prayer requests about how they'd like to change. Together, ask God for wisdom as you each move in new directions...for openness to God's leading...and to be faithful throughout his transformation of your lives.

THE EXORCISM OF EMILY ROSE

Genre: Horror   **Length:** 119 minutes   **Rating:** PG-13

Quick Plot: An agnostic lawyer takes on a negligent homicide case involving a Catholic priest who performed an exorcism on a young girl. Based on a true story.

Why This Movie Is Great for Guys: You may think a horror movie is not appropriate for Christians—but this movie takes a hard look at what it means to believe in God, and it truly challenges viewers to consider their own beliefs.

The transformation of attorney Erin Bruner from an agnostic into someone who might be able to believe in Christ allows for questions about the reality of a supernatural world. The nature of this horror film and the actions of the characters will give men a fresh look at what it means to follow God—regardless of the cost.

FOOD

Hearty Harvest Beef Stew (crock pot)
Sourdough Rolls or French Bread
Drinks (tea, water, soft drinks)
Emily's Autumn Cobbler

 Note: This movie is rated PG-13 for thematic material, including intense, frightening sequences and disturbing images (though there is no excessive gore). It is scary, but the thematic elements are definitely worth exploring.

THE FOOD

Before your event, talk to the guys about dividing up the ingredients and supplies. Keep in mind that some items cost a bit more than others. Maybe two people could share the cost of those ingredients, while others each bring a couple of items.

Easy Option Meal

If you don't own a large crock pot, or if making a cobbler from scratch sounds too ambitious (but we think you can do it!), canned beef stew and pre-made fruit cobblers from the grocery store are good choices for a meal. The movie takes place during a Midwest autumn, so hearty food with good bread is the key.

What you'll need: Names:

Sourdough Rolls or French Bread (serves 8)

1-2 packages sourdough rolls
   or 1-2 loaves French bread   _____

butter   _____

1 garlic clove (peeled)   _____

Emily's Autumn Cobbler (serves 6)

1 large can peaches   _____

1 cup self-rising flour   _____

1 cup sugar   _____

1 cup milk   _____

1 stick butter   _____

½ gallon vanilla ice cream   _____

Hearty Harvest Beef Stew (recipe on page 56)   _____

beverages (tea, water, soft drinks)   _____

Don't forget the napkins, plates, and beverages.

Sourdough Rolls or French Bread

1-2 packages sourdough rolls
–or–
1-2 loaves French bread

butter
1 garlic clove (peeled)

Before heating the sourdough rolls, brush a little melted butter on them, then put them in the oven. If you use French bread, slice the loaf into individual pieces, top with a little butter, and toast them in the oven. While the bread is warm, rub the raw garlic clove on each slice. Serves 8.

Emily's Autumn Cobbler

1 large can peaches
1 cup self rising flour
1 cup sugar

1 cup milk
1 stick butter
½ gallon vanilla ice cream

Melt stick of butter in a microwave (use a microwave safe container), and pour the melted butter into a disposable pan. Pour the canned peaches onto the butter. In a different bowl, mix the flour and sugar together, and then add the milk. Pour this mixture over the peaches. Bake at 350 degrees until the topping is golden brown. Top with vanilla ice cream while warm. Serves 6.

Hearty Harvest Beef Stew (crock pot)

8 potatoes, washed and cut into cubes
8 carrots, washed and cut into pieces
10-ounce package of frozen green beans

4 diced onions
2 pounds lean stew beef, cut into cubes
2 cans cream of mushroom or tomato soup
1 can of brown gravy (optional)

Put all of the ingredients into the crock pot. Add 1½ soup cans of water. Turn the crock pot to low, and let cook for 6 to 8 hours. Serves 8-10.

Making Dinner Happen

You have the home-court advantage here, so make it easy on yourself and have a cooking plan in mind before the event (decide how you'll assign tasks for meal prep). Then, when guests arrive, distribute photocopied recipes and have everyone work together to get the food on the table.

GETTING READY FOR THE SHOW

TalkStarters

Use these questions to prompt discussions as you eat together:
• Have you ever experienced a phenomenon you just couldn't explain—such as a paranormal occurrence? What happened?
• Why do we try so hard to find a rational explanation for things we don't understand?
• What supernatural event from the Bible do you think would make a particularly gripping movie? Do you think Hollywood could do justice to that event? Why or why not?
• What has helped you believe in a God that you can't see? Or what keeps you from believing in God?

The Exorcism of Emily Rose Trivia Quiz

1. How did the idea for this movie originate?
2. This is not actor Colm Feore's first time dabbling with demons on the screen. In which other production did he confront the subject?
3. Director Scott Derrickson is also involved with the remake of a classic science fiction movie featuring the famous line "Gort! Klaatu barada nikto!" What movie is it?
4. This is not Tom Wilkinson's first time playing a priest. What was his other clergy-related role?
5. What sitcom regular was originally considered for the part of Emily Rose?
6. In 2005, Tom Wilkinson played a character on the opposite end of the moral spectrum from his Father Moore character—one who created real problems for a certain billionaire playboy. Who was that character?
7. Actress Mary Beth Hurt (Judge Brewster) also took a turn at campy horror in a 1993 film. What was the film?

Answers
1. The movie is based on the true story of Anneliese Michel, a young German woman who suffered the same fate as the fictional Emily Rose.
2. Colm Feore played the man/demon Andre Linoge in Stephen King's miniseries *Storm of the Century*.
3. *The Day the Earth Stood Still*
4. He played Brother Joseph Dutton in *Molokai: The Story of Father Damien* (2000).
5. *The Nanny's* Madeline Zima was considered for the role.
6. Tom played crime boss Carmine Falcone in *Batman Begins*.
7. She played Mrs. Dingle in *My Boyfriend's Back*.

SHOWTIME!

The Pre-Show

Have everyone gather in the area where you'll show the movie. If you've just finished eating, you may want to provide a quick break for people to use the restroom. When everyone has gathered, serve the peach cobbler and ice cream to those ready for dessert.

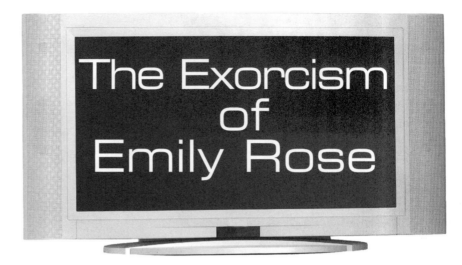

The Exorcism of Emily Rose

Genre: Horror

Length: 119 minutes

Rating: PG-13 for thematic material, including intense, frightening sequences and disturbing images (though there is no excessive gore)

Plot: This movie is the story of a devout young Catholic girl, Emily Rose, who is either suffering from a medical condition such as epilepsy or is being tormented by demons.

When her suffering becomes more than she can bear, and medical treatment offers no relief, Emily turns to her parish priest for help. Upon Emily's desperate request, Father Richard Moore attempts an exorcism—but Emily Rose dies during the violent procedure. The priest is charged with negligent homicide. High-profile defense lawyer Erin Bruner reluctantly agrees to represent Father Moore in exchange for the guarantee of a partnership at her law firm. As the trial progresses, however, Erin's cynicism and agnosticism are challenged by Father Moore's unwavering faith and by the inexplicable events that surround the case. Erin counters the prosecution's claims that Emily was epileptic by challenging the court to consider the possibility that the girl was actually tormented by demons.

Though intense and macabre, this story is relevant: It was inspired by the life of Anneliese Michel, a young woman from Germany who died in 1976 after priests in Wurzburg spent eight months attempting to exorcise demons from her body.

THE POST SHOW

Bible Passages

You may want to use these Bible passages during your movie discussion:

- Matthew 12:28-29

  "But if I drive out demons by the Spirit of God, then the kingdom of God has come upon you. Or again, how can anyone enter a strong man's house and carry off his possessions unless he first ties up the strong man? Then he can rob his house."

- John 6:29

  "Jesus answered, 'The work of God is this: to believe in the one he has sent.' "

- Job 23:10-12

  "But he knows the way that I take; when he has tested me, I will come forth as gold. My feet have closely followed his steps; I have kept to his way without turning aside. I have not departed from the commands of his lips; I have treasured the words of his mouth more than my daily bread."

- Ephesians 5:1-2

  "Be imitators of God, therefore, as dearly loved children and live a life of love, just as Christ loved us and gave himself up for us as a fragrant offering and sacrifice to God."

- Matthew 10:18

  "On my account you will be brought before governors and kings as witnesses to them and to the Gentiles."

Just for Fun!

Got a few extra minutes? Quiz everyone on the following *Emily Rose* movie quotes.

WHO SAID:

- *"What about forgiveness and compassion? Isn't that part of your creed, or does that just get in the way of your work?"*
  (Erin Bruner)

- *"This trial isn't about facts, it's about possibilities."*
  (Erin Bruner)

- *"You're really God's gunslinger, aren't you, Father?"*
  (Ethan Thomas)

- *"Demons exist whether you believe in them or not."*
  (Father Moore)

- *"Once you've looked into the darkness, I think you carry it with you for the rest of your life."*
  (Father Moore)

- *"You're in a spiritual battle, Erin. The forces of darkness are trying to keep you away from the light."*
  (Father Moore)

- *"People say God is dead, but how can they think that if I show them the devil?"*
  (Emily Rose)

DISCUSSION

After the movie, use some or all of these questions to discuss the spiritual themes in *The Exorcism of Emily Rose*.

 If you were on the jury for this court case, which side would you have chosen? Why?

 Do you think there is demon possession in this time in history? Explain your opinion.

Why do you think some people tend to discount the idea that Jesus was both mortal and a supernatural being (man and God)? What are the implications for us today of believing that Jesus was both man and God?

 How did you react to the fact that Emily Rose had the chance to be free from the demons, but chose to continue in her present state until the end?

 Several of the main characters in the movie change over the course of the trial. Discuss which changes you thought were most significant, and why. Did your opinion of what was happening change as the movie progressed as well? If so, explain why.

 The district attorney is portrayed as a "buttoned up, devout churchgoer." Is that the same thing as being a Christian? Explain.

 Director Scott Derrickson is a professing Christian. What message do you think he wants to convey in this movie? Why do you think he never tells the viewer what to believe?

 What lessons can we learn from this movie about the struggle between the natural and the supernatural world?

… about our part in that struggle?

… about the importance of believing in God?

PRAYER

End the evening by closing in prayer, and ask for prayer requests. Begin with a moment of silent prayer, then have each man pray for the man to his left. Close the prayer time by praying for those around us who do not believe—that somehow they may experience God in their lives.

THE END

THE MOVIE
APOLLO 13

Genre: Drama   **Length:** 140 minutes   **Rating:** PG

Quick Plot: This movie is based on the true story of a "routine" lunar mission gone terribly wrong.

Note: This movie is rated PG for language and emotional intensity.

Why This Movie Is Great for Guys: It's the ultimate survival story: Three astronauts stranded 205,000 miles from earth in a crippled spacecraft struggle to return home against seemingly impossible odds. Men will explore themes of leadership, teamwork, and perseverance, and they'll learn that none of us has to face difficulties alone.

FOOD

Stellar Salad
Lift-Off Powered Steaks
Out-of-This-World Baked Potatoes
Galactic Garlic Bread
Easy All-American Apple Pie
Tang

THE FOOD

Before your event, talk to the guys about dividing up the ingredients and supplies. Keep in mind that some items, such as steak, cost a lot more than others. Maybe two people could share the cost of the steak, while others each bring a couple of items.

Easy Option Meal

Some guys have "the right stuff" when it comes to grilling, but some of us are still…well…grill-challenged. If tackling a steak dinner sounds more ambitious than you feel, no worries. In keeping with a particular scene from the movie, substitute with hot dogs, french fries, baked beans (canned are fine), and a store-bought apple pie with ice cream.

Don't forget napkins, plates, steak knives, and forks!

What you'll need: Names:

Stellar Salad (serves 6)

1 head of lettuce or bagged salad greens

vegetables (carrots, cucumbers, and so on)

cheese

croutons

salad dressings (2-3 different kinds)

Lift-Off Powered Steaks

1 steak per person

southwest steak seasoning

Out-of-This-World Baked Potatoes

1 potato per person

butter

sour cream

grated cheese

bacon bits

salt and pepper

Galactic Garlic Bread (serves 8)

1-2 loaves of French bread

garlic powder

butter

vanilla ice cream (for the pie)

Tang

Easy All-American Apple Pie (recipe on page 64)

Stellar Salad

1 head of lettuce or bagged salad
  greens
vegetables such as carrots,
  cucumbers, and radishes, cut into
  small pieces

grated cheese
box of croutons
salad dressings (offer two or three
  different types)

Wash and dry the lettuce or salad greens. Tear lettuce into bite-sized pieces. Put the lettuce/greens into a large bowl. Cut up carrots, cucumbers, or any other salad toppings you like (other good choices are sliced radishes, chopped scallions, or cut-up apples or pears). Put the toppings into individual bowls so people can make their own salads. Sprinkle cheese on top, and keep dressings in the refrigerator until time to serve. Serves 6.

Lift-Off Powered Steaks

1 steak per person
store brand (or homemade) southwest steak seasoning

Rub both sides of each steak with seasoning. Let them sit 10-15 minutes before grilling. (The seasoning will give the steaks that extra "lift-off" power—so be fairly generous with the amount.)

Out-of-This-World
Baked Potatoes

1 potato per person
butter
sour cream

grated cheese
bacon bits
salt and pepper

Rinse and scrub each potato under running water, then dry each potato thoroughly. Pierce each potato deeply with a fork or sharp knife four times on each side at approximately one inch intervals so the steam can escape. Rub butter over the skins, sprinkle the skins with salt, and bake directly on the oven racks until tender (approximately 45 minutes at 400 degrees, 60 minutes at 350 degrees, or 90 minutes at 325 degrees). Have sour cream, cheese, and bacon bits available in individual bowls for toppings. Have salt, pepper, and butter available if anyone wants them.

Galactic Garlic Bread

1-2 loaves French bread
garlic powder
butter

Slice the French bread into individual servings, spread each slice with butter, and sprinkle with garlic powder. Put the bread on a cookie sheet, turn the broiler on high, and place the bread under the broiler until it begins to brown. Be sure to watch the bread because this only takes a minute or two. Can also be done in a toaster oven. Serves 8.

Making Dinner Happen

You have the home-court advantage here, so make it easy on yourself and have a cooking plan in mind before the event (decide how you'll assign tasks for meal prep). Then, when guests arrive, distribute photocopied recipes and have everyone work together to get the food on the table.

Easy All-American Apple Pie

package of two 8-inch pie crusts
1 20-ounce can apple pie filling
½ teaspoon ground cinnamon
½ teaspoon ground allspice
½ teaspoon ground nutmeg

Turn the oven to 425 degrees, and let it preheat about 20 minutes. Separate the two pie pans, and let the crusts thaw for 20 minutes. Mix the apple pie filling, cinnamon, allspice, and nutmeg together. Pour the mixture into one of the pie crusts. Carefully remove the second crust from its pan and place it on top of the first one.

Press the crust around the edge of the pan, and make three small cuts in the top crust. Bake at 425 degrees until crust is golden, 35-40 minutes. Note: Serve with ice cream or slices of cheddar cheese. If you don't have the three spices, it's OK. The filling has plenty of flavor right out of the can. Serves 6-8.

GETTING READY FOR THE SHOW

TalkStarters

Use these questions to prompt discussions as you eat together:
• What is it about space travel that captivates our imaginations so much?
• Tell about a time you were caught in a seemingly hopeless situation (either funny or serious) but were able to make it through with the help of a friend.
• Some astronauts say they've been profoundly changed (including a deepening of their faith), by their trips into space. Tell about an experience you've had that changed you in a big way.
• Why do you think we're often reluctant to accept help from other people, even when we're struggling on our own to no avail?

Apollo 13 Trivia Quiz

1. Ed Harris has also been on the other side of the space capsule. What was his previous space role?
2. The phrase "failure is not an option" is significant in the movie, and it is also the title of Gene Kranz's biography. How many times did the NASA flight director actually use the phrase during the original (actual) mission?
3. Gary Sinise and Tom Hanks have worked together on two other films—one in 1994 and the other in 1999. What were the films?
4. Gary Sinise makes an appearance as CAPCOM at what popular tourist attraction?

5. Which of the actual Apollo 13 astronauts makes a cameo appearance in the movie?

6. The movie is based on the book *Apollo 13* by James Lovell and Jeffrey Kluger, but it was originally published under a different title. What was the original title of the book?

7. Jack Swigert had an interesting financial problem during the ill-fated space flight. What was it (and for extra credit, how did he solve it)?

Answers

1. He played John Glenn in *The Right Stuff*.
2. Never. Gene Kranz never said those words, but he liked the phrase so much, he used them as the title for his biography.
3. *Forest Gump* and *The Green Mile*
4. Mission: Space at Disney World in Orlando
5. James Lovell plays the captain of the USS Iwo Jima.
6. The actual title of the book was *Lost Moon*.
7. Jack Swigert forgot to file his taxes before the flight. (Extra credit answer: President Nixon gave him an extension since Swigert was "out of the country.")

SHOWTIME!

The Pre-Show

Have everyone gather in the area where you'll show the movie. If you've just finished eating, you may want to provide a quick break for people to use the restroom.

Have the pie, ice cream, and beverage refills available for those who want dessert. For authenticity, serve the drink mix that the astronauts used—Tang.

THE SHOW

Genre: Drama

Length: 140 minutes

Rating: PG for language and emotional intensity

Plot: Based on the true story of the near-disastrous Apollo 13 lunar mission, this movie transports us to the time when space travel was still a relatively young venture.

On April 11, 1970, astronauts Jim Lovell, Fred Haise, and Jack Swigert began what was viewed by the world as a routine mission to the moon. But halfway to their destination, an oxygen tank exploded, putting the astronauts in grave danger. They lost oxygen, ran out of power, and were slowly exposed to dangerously high amounts of carbon dioxide.

Suddenly the mission that couldn't even muster routine TV airtime grabbed the national spotlight. Scientists and technicians at Mission Control raced against time to troubleshoot their equipment and to create the solution to a problem thousands of miles away—a problem that meant life or death to the astronauts. The ensuing days tested the courage, faith, and integrity of the space crew, the ground crew, and the families waiting at home.

Just for Fun!

Got a few extra minutes? Quiz everyone on the following *Apollo 13* movie quotes.

WHO SAID:

• *"Houston, we have a problem."*

(Jim Lovell)

• *"If they don't get a break, I don't get a break."*

(Ken Mattingly)

• *"We've never lost an American in space, we're...not gonna lose one on my watch! Failure is not an option."*

(Gene Kranz)

• *(When meeting Neil Armstrong and Buzz Aldrin) "Are you boys in the space program, too?"*

(Blanche Lovell)

• *"No, Henry! Those people don't put one piece of equipment on my lawn. If they have a problem with that, they can take it up with my husband. He'll be home on Friday!"*

(Marilyn Lovell)

• *"Don't you worry. If they could get a washing machine to fly, my Jimmy could land it."*

(Blanche Lovell)

• *"From now on, we live in a world where man has walked on the moon. And it's not a miracle, we just decided to go."*

(Jim Lovell)

• *"I can't deal with cleaning up. Let's sell the house."*

(Marilyn Lovell)

THE POST SHOW

Bible Passages

You may want to use these Bible passages during your movie discussion:

• Philippians 2:1-2

"If you have any encouragement from being united with Christ, if any comfort from his love, if any fellowship with the Spirit, if any tenderness and compassion, then make my joy complete by being like-minded, having the same love, being one in spirit and purpose."

• Romans 8:27-28

"And he who searches our hearts knows the mind of the Spirit, because the Spirit intercedes for the saints in accordance with God's will. And we know that in all things God works for the good of those who love him, who have been called according to his purpose."

• Ecclesiastes 4:9-10

"Two are better than one, because they have a good return for their work: If one falls down, his friend can help him up. But pity the man who falls and has no one to help him up!"

• 1 Corinthians 12:6-7

"There are different kinds of working, but the same God works all of them in all men. Now to each one the manifestation of the Spirit is given for the common good."

DISCUSSION

After the movie, use some or all of these questions to discuss the spiritual themes in *Apollo 13*.

 How did the attitudes of the astronauts contribute to their getting home safely? When do you see your own attitude making a difference in situations? How much of our attitudes are under our own control? Explain your opinion.

Ken Mattingly wanted to fly the mission. How might events have been different had he actually made the flight? Can you relate this to a situation in your own life? If so, share about that time.

 What do Gene Kranz's words "Failure is not an option" mean in your own life? Do you think these words are ones that relate to the Christian life? Explain.

 As the ongoing situation changed, Mission Control had to redefine its actual mission. As growing Christians, are there times when we need to redefine our missions? Explain.

 At one point the news crews wanted to put an antenna on the Lovells' lawn, and Marilyn tells them to take it up with her husband on Friday after he comes home. What does this say to you about faith? When have you had that same kind of faith?

 Teams on land and in space had to think creatively to get through this situation. How does their innovation challenge you to think "bigger"?

 What does this movie help you understand about hope? teamwork?

 What lessons can we learn from this movie about helping others? about accepting help in difficult times?

What better way to end this lunar exploration than with a package of Astronaut Ice Cream for each guest? If it isn't available locally, you can order it from these sources: The Space Store (www.thespacestore.com/asicecream.html) or Kennedy Space Center (www.thespaceshop.com/coandcricecr.html).

PRAYER

Close your time together with prayer requests. Encourage each person to offer a brief prayer that addresses some spiritual truth he has discovered or rediscovered during your time together. Have each person pray for another person in the group, and end the session by praying for the entire group as a whole.

THE END

THE MOVIE
WHAT ABOUT BOB?

Genre: Comedy   **Length:** 99 minutes   **Rating:** PG

Quick Plot: The psychotic, multiphobic patient of a well-known psychiatrist becomes a nuisance while the doctor is on vacation.

☢ Note: This movie has some mild language throughout.

Why This Movie Is Great for Guys: Dr. Marvin's problems with Bob will make guys forget about their own problems—even if it's only for the duration of the film. Guys will explore relational issues with other men and with their own families, they'll evaluate different ways to define success, and they'll enjoy a humorous way to analyze fears or anxieties present in their own lives.

FOOD

Faye's Fried Chicken
Rolls
Not-So-Crazy Corn (on the cob)
Serenity Salad
Drinks (tea, water, soft drinks)
Leo Marvin's Birthday Cake
Ice cream
Gil Crackers (fish-shaped cheese crackers)

THE FOOD

Before your event, talk to the guys about dividing up the ingredients and supplies. Keep in mind that some items, such as chicken, cost more than others. Maybe two people could share the cost of the chicken while others each bring a couple of items.

What you'll need: Names:

Faye's Fried Chicken (serves 8)

8 boneless, skinless
   chicken breasts   _____

2 cups flour   _____

salt and pepper   _____

1 cup milk   _____

vegetable oil for frying   _____

Not-So-Crazy Corn

1 ear of corn per person   _____

butter   _____

salt   _____

1 package of dinner rolls   _____

Serenity Salad (serves 6-8)

1 head of lettuce   _____

tomatoes   _____

cucumbers   _____

salad dressing   _____

**beverages (tea, water,
   soft drinks)**   _____

½ gallon of ice cream   _____

1 birthday cake   _____

fish-shaped cheese crackers   _____

Easy Option Meal

If your group has a cooking phobia, pick up several buckets of chicken from a deli or local chicken takeout restaurant instead. You can usually get rolls, corn, and salads from these locations, too.

Don't forget to provide drinks, napkins, and plates! And if you're serving other than finger foods, be sure to offer silverware as well.

Faye's Fried Chicken

8 boneless, skinless chicken breasts *1 cup of milk*
2 cups of flour *vegetable oil for frying*
salt and pepper

Making Dinner Happen

You have the home-court advantage here, so make it easy on yourself and have a cooking plan in mind before the event (decide how you'll assign tasks for meal prep). Then, when guests arrive, distribute photocopied recipes and have everyone work together to get the food on the table.

In a brown paper bag, mix the flour and about a teaspoon of salt and a teaspoon of pepper (you can adapt those to taste). Heat the oil in a skillet.

Dip a chicken breast into the milk, then drop into the bag with the flour mixture. Shake to coat the chicken, then carefully put the chicken into the hot oil. Repeat with the other pieces of chicken. Fry the chicken about 20 minutes, turning once to make sure it cooks evenly on both sides. Drain on paper towels, then serve on a large plate. Serves 8.

Not-So-Crazy Corn

Remove husks from ears of corn, then rinse corn and place into a large kettle of boiling water. Cook for about 15 minutes. Drain and eat with butter and salt.

Serenity Salad

Use lettuce, tomatoes, and sliced cucumbers to make a tossed salad, or just buy a bag of salad from the produce section of the grocery store. Serve with dressing (just about everyone loves Ranch). Serves 6-8.

Leo Marvin's Birthday Cake

This one is mostly freestyle. Choose any kind of cake you want, but here's the important part: It should be a birthday cake with "Happy Birthday, Doctor Marvin!" written with frosting across the top. We recommend letting your local bakery handle it (don't forget the candles!).

Gil Crackers

Bob Wiley carries his goldfish, Gil, with him everywhere. Fill a fish bowl with fish-shaped cheese crackers. (Your guests will be appreciative if you wash the bowl first.) Write "Gil" on an index card and tape it the side of the bowl.

GETTING READY FOR THE SHOW

TalkStarters

Use these questions to prompt discussions as you eat together:
• What was your favorite vacation ever, and what made it so great?
• What's an extreme thing you've done that might have made others think you were out of your mind (rock climb or rappel? parachute? host a dinner-and-movie event?)
• What's one of your phobias (fear of spiders? airplanes? speaking in front of a crowd?)? In other words, what makes you break out in a sweat?
• People respond to their fears in lots of different ways. What's a goofy thing you'll admit you've done when you were afraid of something?
• Tell about a time your initial impression of someone was wrong— when that person turned out to be different from what you originally thought.

Bill Murray Trivia Quiz

1. In what Bill Murray movie does he relive a single day over and over?
2. In *The Man Who Knew Too Little*, what part of the movie business does Bill Murray's character work in?
3. Between 1977 and 1999, on how many *Saturday Night Live* shows did Murray appear?
4. In what movie is Murray the voice of a cat?
5. What character does Murray play in *Ghostbusters* and *Ghostbusters II*?
6. In what movie does Murray join the army?
7. What's your favorite Bill Murray movie? Why?

Answers
1. *Groundhog Day*
2. Blockbuster Video
3. 77
4. *Garfield*
5. Dr. Pete Venkman
6. *Stripes*

SHOWTIME!

The Pre-Show

Have everyone gather in the area where you'll show the movie. If you've just finished eating, provide a quick break for people to use the restroom.

After everyone is settled, serve cake and ice cream to anyone who's ready for dessert (be sure to pay homage to Dr. Marvin by lighting the candles and singing "Happy Birthday to You" before cutting the cake). Offer Gil Crackers as snacks to devour during the movie.

THE SHOW

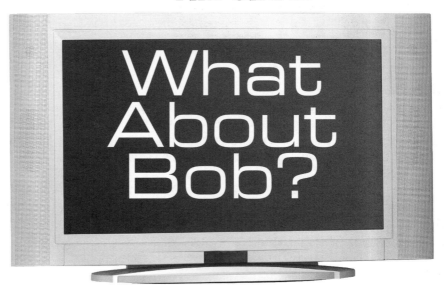

Genre: Comedy

Length: 99 minutes

Rating: PG for some language

Plot: Bob, a man who is bizarrely multiphobic, becomes a patient of well-known psychiatrist Dr. Leo Marvin. Dr. Marvin meets with Bob once, but makes it clear that further appointments will have to wait until he and his family return from their monthlong vacation. This is not good news to Bob, who feels insecure and immediately experiences panic attacks. He is certain that Dr. Marvin is the only one who can help him, so he fakes his own death in order to discover where Dr. Marvin and his family have gone. Imagine Bob's excitement when he and his fish Gil finally disembark from a bus in the Marvin's vacation town. And imagine Dr. Marvin's dismay.

Dr. Marvin uses every trick in his book of psychiatry to get Bob to leave, but Bob is a loyal patient—and a human boomerang. No matter what the doctor tries, Bob comes back—wreaking havoc on the family's vacation and unwittingly revealing the doctor's relational shortcomings. The doctor slowly begins to lose his mind, but what about Bob? Everybody else loves him.

Watch the movie to find out why.

THE POST SHOW

Bible Passages

You may want to use these Bible passages during your movie discussion:

- Psalm 73:26

  "My flesh and my heart may fail, but God is the strength of my heart and my portion forever."

- Psalm 23:4

  "Even though I walk through the valley of the shadow of death, I will fear no evil, for you are with me; your rod and your staff, they comfort me."

- Luke 12:7

  "Indeed, the very hairs of your head are all numbered. Don't be afraid; you are worth more than many sparrows."

- Hebrews 13:6

  "So we say with confidence, 'The Lord is my helper; I will not be afraid. What can man do to me?'"

Just for Fun!

Got a few extra minutes? Quiz everyone on the following quotes from Bill Murray movies. Who said the following (and in what movie):

- *"Don't order the schnitzel, they're using schnauzer."*
  (John Winger in **Stripes**)

- *"I feel good, I feel great, I feel wonderful. I feel good, I feel great, I feel wonderful."*
  (Bob Wiley in **What About Bob?**)

- *"I'll be quiet." "I'll be peace."*
  (Bob Wiley, Sigmund Marvin in **What About Bob?**)

- *"Watch out for that first step, it's a doozy!"*
  (Ned Ryerson in **Groundhog Day**)

- *"Bosley!"*
  (Alex, Natalie, and Dylan; **Charlie's Angels**)

- *"Please don't call me by my real name, it destroys the reality I'm trying to create."*
  (Wallace "Wally" Ritchie in **The Man Who Knew Too Little**)

DISCUSSION

After the movie, use some or all of these questions to discuss the spiritual themes in *What About Bob?*

 Do you know anyone like Bob? If you do, how do you interact with this person? How could Dr. Marvin have better handled his situation with Bob?

 Can a vacation really take us away from our problems? Why or why not?

 Do you think the idea of taking "baby steps" would help you deal with your own problems? Explain.

 Dr. Marvin is driven to insanity by Bob. Do you believe other people can cause us to behave irrationally? How can we avoid a situation like that?

How would you describe Dr. Marvin's relationship with his family? What does Bob seem to understand about priorities that the doctor hasn't figured out yet? How do we, as men, sometimes make the same mistakes that Dr. Marvin makes in the movie?

 Bob and Siggy both are afraid of dying. Why do you think some Christians are still afraid of death?

 How can a relationship with God help us overcome worries or fears?

 How can we put lessons learned from this movie to use in our own daily lives?

PRAYER

End the night with a prayer. Ask everyone for prayer requests, then allow volunteers to take turns praying aloud for each member of the group. Ask God to help each of you become the best example of Jesus' love to others and to use wisdom in setting priorities in your daily lives.

THE END

THE MOVIE

THE LORD OF THE RINGS: THE FELLOWSHIP OF THE RI

Genre: Fantasy   **Length:** 178 minutes (theatrical version)   **Rating:** PG-13

Quick Plot: A young hobbit must dispose of an evil talisman that he involuntarily inherits, but the task is more difficult than he'd imagined.

Why This Movie Is Great for Guys: This is the ultimate epic fantasy about bravery and heroism. Ordinary people are called upon to do extraordinary things—a wonderful illustration of the spiritual conflicts in our own world.

 Note: This movie is rated PG-13 for battle sequences and scary images (violent fantasy battles, monsters).

FOOD

Camp-Cooked Harvest Fruit
Hobbit Mushroom Basket
Haunch of Meat on a Bun
Misty Mountains Strawberry Pie
Drinks (soda, water, tea, cider)

THE FOOD

Before your event, talk to the guys about dividing up the ingredients and supplies. Keep in mind that some items, such as ground buffalo, cost a bit more than others. Perhaps two people would like to share the cost of the burgers, while others each bring a couple of items.

Easy Option Meal

If your group doesn't feel like cooking, pick up an easy country meal of roasted chicken and a few sides from your local deli restaurant or your supermarket's deli counter.

Don't forget to provide napkins, silverware, and plates! And why not entertain as a hobbit likely would? Rustic is key.

What you'll need: Names:

Hobbit Mushroom Basket (serves 8)

16 large button mushrooms _____

¼ cup olive oil _____

2 cloves garlic, minced _____

dash cayenne _____

Haunch of Meat on a Bun (serves 8)

3 pounds ground buffalo or
   lean ground beef _____

¼ cup Worcestershire sauce _____

½ cup barbecue sauce _____

8 strips center-cut bacon _____

1 avocado _____

salt and pepper _____

8 hamburger buns _____

preferred toppings (tomato, onion,
   lettuce, cheese, ketchup, mustard) _____

**beverages (soda, water,
   tea, cider)** _____

**Camp-Cooked Harvest
Fruit (recipe on page 77)** _____

**Misty Mountains
Strawberry Pie (recipe
on page 77)** _____

Hobbit Mushroom Basket

16 large button mushrooms
¼ cup olive oil

2 cloves garlic, minced
dash cayenne

Toss mushrooms with oil and spices. Place them in the middle of a large piece of heavy-duty foil. Fold the ends together, leaving some room inside for air circulation. Grill over medium heat 8-10 minutes until tender. Serves 8.

Haunch of Meat on a Bun

3 pounds ground buffalo or lean
   ground beef
¼ cup Worcestershire sauce
½ cup barbecue sauce
8 strips center-cut bacon

1 avocado
salt and pepper
8 hamburger buns
preferred toppings (tomato, onion,
   lettuce, cheese, ketchup, mustard)

Prepare your toppings, and slice the avocado. Mix the meat with the Worcestershire sauce, and form into burgers; season both sides with salt and pepper. Grill over high heat, 4-5 minutes per side for medium. Cook the bacon until crisp in a pan or in the microwave (or on the grill if it isn't too fatty). One minute before the burgers are done, brush them with the barbecue sauce. Put everything together, topping your burgers with the avocado, bacon, and whatever else you want. Serves 8.

Camp-Cooked Harvest Fruit

4 plums
4 small oranges
4 peaches

4 tablespoons sugar
8 metal skewers or wooden skewers
   soaked in water for 20 minutes

Cut the pieces of fruit in half and thread a piece of each onto each skewer with the cut sides facing up flat. Sprinkle the sugar onto the cut sides of the fruit and let it soak in. Refrigerate until cooking time. Cook at the same time as the mushrooms. Spray the grill with nonstick spray, and grill the skewers cut side down for 5 minutes, until heated through. Serves 8.

Misty Mountains Strawberry Pie

1 pre-made graham cracker crust
½ gallon container of vanilla bean
   ice cream

2 containers frozen sliced
   strawberries, presweetened
½ teaspoon cinnamon

Thaw the strawberries in the microwave, and drain some of their juice. Mix the cinnamon into strawberries. Slightly soften the ice cream, and scoop it out into a large mixing bowl. Fold in the strawberries, but don't overmix. Scoop the mixture into the crust, cover with plastic wrap and store in the freezer. Allow at least 4 hours for hardening, then remove from the freezer at least 5 minutes before serving. Serves 8.

Making Dinner Happen

You have the home-court advantage here, so make it easy on yourself and have a cooking plan in mind before the event (decide how you'll assign tasks for meal prep). Then, when guests arrive, distribute photocopied recipes and have everyone work together to get the food on the table.

GETTING READY FOR THE SHOW

TalkStarters

Use these questions to prompt discussions as you eat together:

• *The Hobbit* was a best-selling novel during the '70s, and then it became an award-winning movie several decades later. What other books can you think of that evolved into successful films? Which is your favorite, and why?

• Why do you think people enjoy books and movies of fantasy?

• Tolkien probably had a lot of fun creating the fantasy world of his *Hobbit* saga. If you could create a world of your own imagination, what would it look like?

• Tell about a time you were called upon to accomplish a task that seemed daunting or even risky.

The Lord of the Rings Trivia Quiz

1. About how long did it take J.R.R. Tolkien to write *The Lord of the Rings*?
2. How much were the film rights for *The Lord of the Rings* sold for?
3. What literary discussion group was J.R.R. Tolkien a part of during the writing of *The Lord of the Rings*? For bonus points, name some of its other associates.
4. Christopher Lee, who plays the treacherous Saruman in *The Fellowship of the Rings*, also played which of these other famous villains?
   A. Count Dooku
   B. Dracula
   C. Francisco Scaramanga (*The Man With the Golden Gun*)
5. What rank did *The Lord of the Rings* achieve in Amazon.com's "Book of the Millennium" poll?
   A. 1st
   B. 15th
   C. 123rd
6. Howard Shore, the composer for *The Lord of the Rings*, began his composition career on what famous TV show?
7. In what country was J.R.R. Tolkien born?

Answers
1. 12 years (1937-1949)
2. Tolkien sold them for $15,000 in 1968.
3. The Inklings, which also included C.S. Lewis, Warren Lewis, Charles Williams, Owen Barfield, and Hugo Dyson.
4. All of them. He also played Fu Manchu, Frankenstein's monster, and the mummy.
5. A. 1st. It was also voted best-loved book and best book of the 20th century in major polls in Britain and Australia.
6. *Saturday Night Live*
7. South Africa. He was raised in England after his father's death, though, and spent his teenage years in the care of a priest after his mother died.

SHOWTIME!

The Pre-Show

Have everyone gather in the area where you'll show the movie. If you've just finished eating, you may want to provide a quick break for people to use the restroom.

THE SHOW

Genre: Fantasy

Length: 178 minutes

Rating: PG-13 for battle sequences and some scary images

Plot: Hobbit Frodo Baggins is shocked when he discovers that the magic ring he's recently inherited is the master ring of the dark lord Sauron. If Sauron regains it, nothing will be able to stop him from covering the world in darkness. And unless it is destroyed, Sauron can never be defeated.

Frodo and his loyal friends find themselves white-knuckling it through one predicament after another as they evade, outwit, and ultimately battle the servants of the dark lord bent on recovering the ring. But how can the naturally passive hobbits combat darkness... and win?

THE POST SHOW

Bible Passages

You may want to use these Bible passages during your movie discussion:

• **1 Samuel 16:7**

"But the Lord said to Samuel, 'Do not consider his appearance or his height, for I have rejected him. The Lord does not look at the things man looks at. Man looks at the outward appearance, but the Lord looks at the heart.' "

• **1 Corinthians 1:26-29**

"Brothers, think of what you were when you were called. Not many of you were wise by human standards; not many were influential; not many were of noble birth. But God chose the foolish things of the world to shame the wise; God chose the weak things of the world to shame the strong. He chose the lowly things of this world and the despised things—and the things that are not—to nullify the things that are, so that no one may boast before him."

• **Judges 6:15-16**

" 'But Lord,' Gideon asked, 'how can I save Israel? My clan is the weakest in Manasseh, and I am the least in my family!' The Lord answered, 'I will be with you, and you will strike down all the Midianites together.' "

• **Joshua 1:7**

"Be strong and very courageous. Be careful to obey all the law my servant Moses gave you; do not turn from it to the right or to the left, that you may be successful wherever you go."

DISCUSSION

After the movie, use some or all of these questions to discuss the spiritual themes in *The Fellowship of the Ring*.

 Who do you see as the hero of *The Lord of the Rings: The Fellowship of the Ring*? Who do you appreciate or identify with the most? Why? What do you think there is to learn from that character's story or example?

 In their pivotal battle against darkness, nine people from different backgrounds and cultures banded together in order to defeat the enemy. Was there ever a time you had to work within a diverse group in order to achieve a common goal? What happened?

Tell about a time you, like Bilbo, had something in your life that you refused to surrender—even though you knew you should. How did you get rid of it—if you did?

 If you were in Frodo's position, would you have gone on this quest? Explain.

 Why do you think Tolkien chose hobbits as the heroes for his great mythic adventure? How is this important to the story and its message?

 What kind of leader does Aragorn represent? How is he an example to us as men?

 Why would Frodo have been chosen to bear the ring when others were probably more capable? What do such examples (in stories and real life) reveal about our expectations compared to God's?

 Why do you think it was so tempting for Boromir to put his trust in the power of the ring for victory? Do you ever find that your own strength is a hindrance to putting your trust in God? Explain.

 In your opinion, what message is most strongly conveyed at the end of this movie? How does the story's open ending affect your perception of the message?

PRAYER

Close the evening with a prayer. Ask for prayer requests if you have time, and have volunteers take turns praying for the group. Remember to pray that God would find ways to use you and would give you courage and strength to serve him even when you don't think you're adequate.

THE END

THE BOURNE IDENTITY

Genre: Action   **Length:** 119 minutes   **Rating:** PG-13

Quick Plot: A victim of amnesia, Jason Bourne isn't sure who he is. Racing against government agents who know his actual identity, Bourne must piece clues together—before he loses himself forever.

Note: This movie is rated PG-13 for language and violence. There are also scenes of blood, drinking, gunfights, and sexual scenes without nudity.

Why This Movie Is Great for Guys: It's not tame stuff. A man runs for his life in a thrilling, mind-bending chase, and guys will get caught up in the labyrinth of clues that Bourne must solve in order to survive. Themes of the movie will prompt us to identify those things that define us and that shape others' perceptions of who we are.

FOOD

Sailor's Goulash
Basic Breakfast: Eggs, Toast, and Bacon
(Breakfast is good any time of day!)
Coffee
Breakfast Pastries

THE FOOD

Before your event, talk to the guys about dividing up the ingredients and supplies. Keep in mind that some items, such as breakfast pastries, cost a little more than others. Maybe two people could share the cost of those items, while others each bring a couple of ingredients.

What you'll need: Names:

Basic Breakfast

2-3 eggs per person   _____

1 loaf bread   _____

1-2 packages bacon   _____

butter   _____

assorted jams   _____

Breakfast Pastries (serves 6-12)

Combine the following to
   make 1 dozen: _____

doughnuts   _____

muffins   _____

bagels   _____

cream cheese   _____

**Sailor's Goulash
(recipe on page 84)**   _____

coffee   _____

Easy Option Meal

If your group doesn't exactly identify with the kitchen, no worries—the movie opens with a fishing trawler in the Mediterranean Sea, so why not continue the maritime theme with seafood? Check out your supermarket deli for ready-made seafood pasta salad, thaw a tray of frozen shrimp, and finish up with a store-bought dessert. Presto! Dinner is as good as served.

Somehow, Jason Bourne forgot who he was. You might forget the napkins and silverware for this Dinner and a Movie event. There's a connection here—and we're confident that you'll figure it out.

2-3 eggs per person
1-2 packages bacon
1 loaf bread

butter
assorted jams

This recipe is aptly named: It's really just a basic breakfast. Fry, poach, or scramble the eggs; fry the bacon; and toast the bread (offer butter and jam for the toast). Pretty easy, eh?

■ *Sailor's Goulash*

1 pound hamburger
1 medium onion, chopped
1 can cream of mushroom soup
1 soup can of milk

1 package Tater Tots frozen
   potatoes
1 bag of frozen vegetables

Mix hamburger, chopped onion, and vegetables. Place in casserole dish. Place Tater Tots on top. Mix milk and soup together. Pour over top. Bake 350 degrees for 1 hour and 15 minutes. Serves 6.

GETTING READY FOR THE SHOW

TalkStarters

Use these questions to prompt discussions as you eat together:
• Is there special significance to any part of your name (first, middle, or last)? Explain.
• Tell us about your family heritage. Which part of this heritage do you identify with most?
• What place, type of food, or music reminds you of your roots? In what way?
• Everyone place your driver's license or other picture ID on the table. Do any of the pictures surprise you? Why or why not?
• If you were going on a lengthy road trip, who would you most want to accompany you?
• Describe yourself in five words.

The Bourne Identity/Matt Damon Trivia Quiz

1. Who authored the book that this movie was based on?
2. What's Matt Damon's hometown?
3. What university did Matt Damon attend?
4. What 1997 movie did Matt Damon star in and co-author?
5. How much money did *The Bourne Identity* generate at U.S. box offices?

Answers
1. Robert Ludlum
2. Cambridge, Massachusetts
3. Harvard University
4. *Good Will Hunting*
5. $121,661,683

SHOWTIME!

The Pre-Show

Have everyone gather in the area where you'll show the movie. If you've just finished eating, you may want to provide a quick break for people to use the restroom.

When everyone has gathered, serve the breakfast pastries and coffee or other beverage. Be sure to provide napkins.

THE SHOW

Genre: Action

Length: 119 minutes

Rating: PG-13 for language and violence. There are also scenes of blood, drinking, gunfights, and sex scenes without nudity.

Plot: We're invested in this movie from the start as we—along with Jason Bourne—struggle to unravel the mystery of who he is and why he's discovered floating in the sea with gunshot wounds. Rescued by sailors, Jason embarks on a dangerous journey to solve the puzzle that is his life.

There are clues to help him—and us. We know that a safety deposit box exists for him with passports, money, and a gun. We see that he possesses a unique set of survival skills such as climbing, fighting, tying ropes, speaking a variety of languages, and reading dangerous situations.

He has no friends...that is, until he meets Marie. Agreeing to give him a lift one day, her life changes forever as she becomes involved with Jason and his struggle for identity.

Ah—we've forgotten one detail: The government knows who Jason Bourne is, and will do anything necessary to bring him in dead or alive.

But why?

Just for Fun!

Got a few extra minutes? Quiz everyone on the following *Bourne Identity* movie quotes.

WHO SAID:

• *"I do not know who I am. Tell me who I am."*
  (Jason Bourne)

• *"You're asking me a direct question? I thought that you were never going to do that."*
  (Alexander Conklin)

• *"Look. You drive. I pay. It's that simple."*
  (Jason Bourne)

• *"I want Bourne in a body bag by sundown."*
  (Alexander Conklin)

• *"How could I forget about you? You're the only person I know."*
  (Jason Bourne)

• *"It says I'm an assassin."*
  (Jason Bourne)

• *"I don't want to know who I am anymore. I don't care. Everything I've found out I want to forget. I don't care who I am or what I did."*
  (Jason Bourne)

• *"You're U.S. government property. You're a malfunctioning $30 million weapon."*
  (Alexander Conklin)

• *"I don't want to do this anymore."*
  (Jason Bourne)

• *"Shut it down."*
  (Ward Abbott)

THE POST SHOW

Bible Passages

You may want to use these Bible passages during your movie discussion:

• Romans 8:17

  "Now if we are children, then we are heirs—heirs of God and co-heirs with Christ, if indeed we share in his sufferings in order that we may also share in his glory."

• Colossians 3:12

  "Therefore, as God's chosen people, holy and dearly loved, clothe yourselves with compassion, kindness, humility, gentleness and patience."

• Psalm 139:7

  "Where can I go from your Spirit? Where can I flee from your presence?"

• John 1:12

  "Yet to all who received him, to those who believed in his name, he gave the right to become children of God."

DISCUSSION

After the movie, use some or all of these questions to discuss the spiritual themes in *The Bourne Identity*.

 At the beginning of the movie, Jason is rescued from the sea—saved from what might have been a hopeless situation. Tell about a time in your life you were rescued.

 If we had to rely on clues in your life that might point to your identity, what clues would be most helpful to us? Why?

What clues should be evident in our lives that might show others that we're Christians? Can you back up your thoughts with Scripture?

 It seemed as though Jason Bourne was constantly reeling from life's "punches," but he never stopped fighting for survival. How quickly do you recover when life delivers you a punch? What tactics do you use to survive?

 Jason couldn't seem to escape surveillance—even cameras that caught snapshots of him with Marie. How is that like or unlike having an omniscient God who knows everything about us? How do you feel about God knowing everything you do?

 As Jason Bourne discovers who he is, he doesn't like what he finds. Is there anything about yourself that you wish you could change? What are the things you would never want to change?

 Those close to Jason Bourne are impacted as he begins to recapture his identity. How can you impact the people around you as you live out your identity in Christ?

PRAYER

End the evening by praying together. First, ask for prayer requests. Then encourage each person to share one specific way he'll apply the lessons learned from the movie *The Bourne Identity*. Try a method of "popcorn prayers" to have each person pray for someone else in the group; for example, guys can offer short sentence prayers aloud whenever they feel led.

THE MOVIE
X-MEN

Genre: Action   **Length:** 104 minutes   **Rating:** PG-13

Quick Plot: Super-powered mutants are living among us! Some people believe the mutants must be monitored and controlled. Others are willing to die to prevent that—and some are willing to kill. The war is coming...

Why This Movie Is Great for Guys: Superheroes fighting super-villains! Conflicting philosophies of the main characters will help men think about how they choose to use their own abilities.

 Note: This movie is rated PG-13 for sci-fi action violence. There is also mild sensuality in the form of a scantily clad shape-shifter.

FOOD

New York Hot Dogs
X-Logo Tomatoes
Big Apple Rice Salad
Drinks (soda, ice water)
NY Cheesecake

THE FOOD

Before your event, talk to the guys about dividing up the ingredients and supplies. Keep in mind that some items, such as the cheesecake, cost a lot more than others. Maybe two people could share the cost of the cheesecake, while others each bring a couple of items.

What you'll need: Names:

New York Hot Dogs (serves 8)

2 packages all-beef hot dogs   _____

2 packages hot dog buns   _____

1 jar Dijon mustard   _____

2 medium white onions   _____

1 tablespoon vegetable oil   _____

½ cup ketchup   _____

⅓ cup sweet barbecue sauce   _____

8 ounces asiago or (real)
  parmesan cheese   _____

X-Logo Tomatoes (serves 8)

8 small tomatoes   _____

½ cup Italian dressing   _____

6 mozzarella cheese sticks
  (string cheese)   _____

4 tablespoons grated or shredded
  Parmesan cheese   _____

basil   _____

foil tray, tinfoil, or grilling basket   _____

NY Cheesecake (serves 8)

1 store-bought plain cheesecake   _____

1 jar strawberry sundae topping   _____

beverages (soda, ice water)   _____

Big Apple Rice Salad
(recipe on page 90)   _____

Easy Option Meal

If your group doesn't feel like cooking, pick up an easy meal of New York–style food, such as thin-crust pizza or microwave hot dogs, and pick up a few bags of chips (and a cheesecake, naturally!).

Don't forget the cups, napkins, and other basic supplies. If you're going with paper plates and dinnerware, white would be appropriate for the urban simplicity of New York street food.

2 packages all-beef hot dogs
2 packages hot dog buns
1 jar Dijon mustard
2 medium white onions
1 tablespoon vegetable oil

½ cup ketchup
⅓ cup sweet barbecue sauce
8 ounces asiago or (real) Parmesan cheese (check the deli section of your supermarket)

Making Dinner Happen

You have the home-court advantage here, so make it easy on yourself and have a cooking plan in mind before the event (decide how you'll assign tasks for meal prep). Then, when guests arrive, distribute photocopied recipes and have everyone work together to get the food on the table.

Dice the onions and sauté in the oil in a medium saucepan over medium heat until soft. Add ketchup and barbecue sauce, stir. Let cool. Grill the hot dogs until done, serve on buns with mustard and onion sauce. Crumble a little cheese over the top of each one. Serves 8.

X-Logo Tomatoes

8 small tomatoes (vine-ripened)
½ cup Italian dressing
6 mozzarella cheese sticks (string cheese)
4 tablespoons grated or shredded

Parmesan cheese (fresh preferred)
basil
foil tray, tinfoil, or grilling basket

Preheat grill to medium high heat. Slice tomatoes in half and arrange face-up in foil tray. Brush or drizzle tomatoes with dressing, sprinkle with Parmesan cheese and basil. Peel string cheese into strips, place 2 strips crosswise on top of tomatoes, making an X on each. Grill until cheese is melted and bottoms are just browned, 10-12 minutes. Serves 8.

NY Cheesecake

1 plain cheesecake
1 jar strawberry sundae topping

Making authentic cheesecake is a pretty complex undertaking (not that we doubt your culinary abilities), so your best bet is to buy one from a local supermarket or restaurant. That said, here's the recipe: Remove cheesecake from box. Drizzle strawberry topping over all. Serves 8.

Big Apple Rice Salad

1 cup instant rice, uncooked
½ cup pineapple or coconut low-fat yogurt
1 cup frozen whipped topping (thawed)

1 apple (gala, cameo, pink lady, or fuji)
1 cup seedless grape halves
1 pear (canned or fresh)
½ teaspoon cinnamon

Cook the rice according to the directions on the package. Rinse and drain. Mix yogurt and cinnamon, and fold in whipped topping. Cut up the fruit into small chunks. Mix ingredients, and refrigerate until ready to serve. Serves 8.

GETTING READY FOR THE SHOW

TalkStarters

Use these questions to prompt discussions as you eat together:

• If you could have any superpower, what would it be? Why?
• Have you ever found yourself identifying with or sympathizing with a movie's villain? Who was it? Why did you respond that way?
• Tell about a time you experienced some sort of prejudice—on the receiving end or otherwise. What did you learn from that experience?
• Have you ever been afraid to reveal your "real" self because you were afraid of how people would react? Explain.
• Why do you think people are so attracted to the idea of superheroes and superpowers?

X-Men Trivia Quiz

1. Explain how the following superheroes got their powers: Spider-Man, The Fantastic Four, the X-Men, Superman, Blade, Daredevil.
2. Who were the five original X-men? For bonus points, list their real names as well.
3. As of 2007, what is the highest-grossing movie based on a comic book?
4. As of 2007, which of the following awards has Hugh Jackman *not* won?
   A. A Tony
   B. An Oscar
   C. An Emmy
   D. A People's Choice Award
5. What other famous Marvel franchises have been made into major motion pictures?
6. Where does Cyclops get the energy for his optic beam?
   A. The sun
   B. Cosmic radiation
   C. The electromagnetic field of the earth

Answers

1. Bite from a genetically modified spider, cosmic rays, DNA mutation, he's an alien, he's half vampire, toxic waste
2. Cyclops (Scott Summers), Angel (Warren Worthington III), Beast (Hank McCoy), Iceman (Bobby Drake), and Marvel Girl (Jean Grey)
3. *Spider-Man*, at over $403 million
4. An Oscar or People's Choice Award
5. Spiderman, Daredevil, The Fantastic Four (just to name a few).
6. The sun

SHOWTIME!

The Pre-Show

Have everyone gather in the area where you'll show the movie. If you've just finished eating, you may want to provide a quick break for people to use the restroom. And by the way—now is the perfect time for a "name the ultimate mutant" election. Have everyone list mutants (from memory or from the *X-Men* movies), and cast your votes for the ultimate mutant!

THE SHOW

Genre: Action

Length: 104 minutes

Rating: PG-13 for sci-fi action violence (no gore)

Plot: The world is still coping with the revelation that there are mutants—people with potentially dangerous and controversial powers—living among us. Many people believe that the only solution for non-mutant security is to force mutants to register with the federal government, and they're determined to see that proposition made into law.

Estranged mutant friends Professor Charles Xavier and Magneto both oppose the Mutant Registration Act and resolve to defeat it. But where Xavier believes in cooperation and peaceful means, Magneto is willing to do anything to achieve his ends.

Caught in the middle of the conflict are two runaway mutants, Rogue and Wolverine, doggedly pursued by Magneto for unknown reasons. If he isn't stopped quickly, Magneto will take control, instigating a war that can only end in devastation for everyone.

THE POST SHOW

Bible Passages

You may want to use these Bible passages during your movie discussion:

- 1 Corinthians 12:4-7

  "There are different kinds of gifts, but the same Spirit. There are different kinds of service, but the same Lord. There are different kinds of working, but the same God works all of them in all men. Now to each one the manifestation of the Spirit is given for the common good."

- 1 Peter 4:10

  "Each one should use whatever gift he has received to serve others, faithfully administering God's grace in its various forms."

- Matthew 5:9

  "Blessed are the peacemakers, for they will be called sons of God."

- Jonah 4:2

  "He prayed to the Lord, 'O Lord, is this not what I said when I was still at home? That is why I was so quick to flee to Tarshish. I knew that you are a gracious and compassionate God, slow to anger and abounding in love, a God who relents from sending calamity.' "

- 1 Corinthians 13:1-3

  "If I speak in the tongues of men and of angels, but have not love, I am only a resounding gong or a clanging cymbal. If I have the gift of prophecy and can fathom all mysteries and all knowledge, and if I have a faith that can move mountains, but have not love, I am nothing. If I give all I possess to the poor and surrender my body to the flames, but have not love, I gain nothing."

Just for Fun!

Got a few extra minutes? Quiz everyone on the following *X-Men* movie quotes.

WHO SAID:

- *"It's a war. It's the reason people like me exist."*

  (Senator Kelly)

- *"Let's just say God works too slowly."*

  (Magneto)

- *"You Homo sapiens and your guns."*

  (Magneto)

- *"The whole world out there is full of people that hate and fear you, and you're wasting your time trying to protect them."*

  (Wolverine)

- *"Your sacrifice will mean our survival. I'll understand if that comes as small consolation."*

  (Magneto)

- *"What would you prefer, yellow spandex?"*

  (Cyclops)

- *"Don't you people ever die?"*

  (Toad)

- *"The war is still coming, Charles, and I intend to fight it, by any means necessary." "And I will always be there, old friend."*

  (Magneto, Prof. Xavier)

DISCUSSION

After the movie, use some or all of these questions to discuss the spiritual themes in *X-Men*.

 How did Wolverine's beliefs change over the course of this movie? When have you had your beliefs change significantly, and what brought that about?

Was there anything wrong with Wolverine's initial decision not to use his abilities for either side? Why or why not? If we have the ability to make a difference, are we obligated to use those abilities? Explain.

 Does your personality most reflect Magneto (the end justifies the means), Wolverine (look out for number one), or Xavier (always under moral constraints)? Explain.

 Which one of the X-Men has characteristics most similar to those you would associate with a Christian? Explain your thoughts, and see if you can back them up with Scripture.

 What made it justifiable for the X-Men to resort to fighting? Should they have killed Magneto? Why or why not?

 Do you ever wish God were more like Magneto (just hurry up and...well...smite something)? Why or why not? What do you think the world would be like if God were more like this?

 The mutants had abilities they could use for good or for evil. What are abilities God has given you? How are you using those right now? How could you better use these abilities?

 What message does this movie convey about how we should use our unique abilities?

PRAYER

Take time to close the evening in prayer. Go around the circle and take prayer requests. Remember to ask for God's blessing on you as a team of believers and for his help in developing and using your gifts.

THE END

THE MOVIE

ESCAPE FROM ALCATRAZ

Genre: Drama/Thriller   **Length:** 111 minutes   **Rating:** PG

Quick Plot: Four prison inmates collaborate on a complex scheme to break from Alcatraz Federal Penitentiary. Based on a true story.

Why This Movie Is Great for Guys: Great risks and impossible odds! The theme of life's meaning along with the pursuit of freedom will challenge men to wrestle with their understanding of what freedom is and how it's lived out.

 Note: This movie is rated PG for occasional strong language, violence, brief nudity (naked prisoners, seen from behind, walking into a shower room), and thematic elements relating to prison life.

FOOD

You-Do-the-Work Chicken and Rice
Prison Cafeteria Fruit Salad
Drinks (soda, iced tea, or water)
No-Frills Ice-Cream Sandwiches

THE FOOD

Before your event, talk to the guys about dividing up the ingredients and supplies. Keep in mind that some items, such as chicken, cost a lot more than others. Maybe two people could share the cost of the chicken, while others each bring a couple of items.

Easy Option Meal

If your group doesn't feel like cooking, order in a few pizzas or bake frozen pizzas. Be sure to provide a choice of different toppings.

Remember the drinks, plates, cups, napkins, and spoons (no knives or forks for this one—not allowed in prison!).

What you'll need: Names:

You-Do-the-Work Chicken and Rice (serves 8)

4 cups instant rice _____

4 chicken breast halves _____

2 large cans chow mein noodles _____

2 large cans crushed pineapple and juice, heated _____

3 cups slivered almonds _____

2 cups coconut _____

6 stalks celery, sliced _____

2 small onions, chopped _____

4 cups cheddar cheese, grated _____

2 cans cream of chicken soup _____

Prison Cafeteria Fruit Salad (serves 8)

2 large cans mixed chopped fruit _____

2 cups miniature marshmallows _____

1 container frozen whipped topping _____

beverages (soda, iced tea, water) _____

1 ice-cream sandwich per person _____

96

You-Do-the-Work Chicken and Rice

4 cups instant rice
4 chicken breast halves
2 large cans chow mein noodles
2 large cans crushed pineapple with juice, heated
3 cups slivered almonds

2 cups coconut
6 stalks celery, sliced
2 small onions, chopped
4 cups cheddar cheese, grated
2 cans cream of chicken soup

Cut the chicken into small cubes and place into a pot. Fill the pot with water until chicken is covered. Bring water to a boil, and cook chicken until tender. Drain the water. Prepare the rice according to the instructions on the package. To make gravy, prepare the chicken soup according to the instructions on the can (add less water for thicker gravy).

Place each of the ingredients in its own bowl. Each person assembles his own meal by putting the desired amount of rice on a plate, adding the other ingredients on top as desired, and finishing with the gravy. Serves 8.

Making Dinner Happen

You have the home-court advantage here, so make it easy on yourself and have a cooking plan in mind before the event (decide how you'll assign tasks for meal prep). Then, when guests arrive, distribute photocopied recipes and have everyone work together to get the food on the table.

Prison Cafeteria Fruit Salad

2 large cans mixed chopped fruit
2 cups miniature marshmallows

1 container frozen whipped topping (thawed)

Don't let the name keep you from serving this salad—it's as good as it is easy! Here's all you do: Drain liquid from cans of fruit, and dump fruit into a large serving bowl. Add about 2 cups marshmallows, then fold enough whipped topping into the mix to evenly coat the fruit. If possible, chill before serving. Serves 8.

GETTING READY FOR THE SHOW

TalkStarters

Use these questions to prompt discussions as you eat together:

• Name at least one other "prison movie" you've seen. Now name another movie with escape as part of the plot.

• Alcatraz was a pretty gloomy place—let's put a spin on the whole idea of island incarceration. Imagine that you're exiled to an island of your choice under living conditions of your choosing. Where would you go? Describe what your life would be like on that island.

• Inmates aren't allowed many personal items. Which personal item would you most hate to do without if you were behind bars?

• Describe a time you felt as though your freedom were restricted in some way. How did you respond to the situation?

• What does freedom mean to you? What does it look like in day-to-day life?

Alcatraz Trivia Quiz

1. During what years did Alcatraz operate as a federal prison?
2. Where did the name *Alcatraz* come from?
3. Name three famous Alcatraz inmates.
4. How and when was Alcatraz Island first used by the U.S. government?
5. How many escape attempts have been made from Alcatraz Federal Penitentiary?

Answers
1. 1934-1963
2. It's Spanish for "Island of Pelicans."
3. Al Capone, Alvin "Creepy Karpis" Karpowicz, George Barnes (aka George "Machine Gun" Kelly), Joe Cretzer, Robert Stroud (aka "The Birdman of Alcatraz")
4. As a federal fort in 1859.
5. Fourteen attempts involving 36 prisoners. Of those who tried, 23 were caught, 7 died from gunfire, 2 drowned, and 4 were never found.

SHOWTIME!

The Pre-Show

Have everyone gather in the area where you'll show the movie. If you've just finished eating, you might want to provide a quick break for people to use the restroom.

Before starting the movie, make sure everyone has enough to drink, and distribute the ice-cream sandwiches along with napkins. Ask if anyone in the group has ever visited Alcatraz. If so, ask them to share about their experience. If not, imagine—as a group—what it might be like to visit there.

THE SHOW

Escape From Alcatraz

Genre: Drama/Thriller

Length: 111 minutes

Rating: PG for fight scenes (inmates physically assaulting one another), brief gore (an inmate chopping off his own fingers), some brief nudity (naked prisoners, seen from behind, walking into a shower room, and thematic elements relating to prison life (an inmate making a sexual advance on another inmate)

Plot: Clint Eastwood stars as Frank Morris, a tough convict with a brilliant mind and a penchant for breaking out of prisons.

Having disappeared one too many times, Morris is moved to Alcatraz—a maximum-security prison from which no one has ever escaped. Once on "The Rock," he encounters a strict warden and a colorful cast of inmates—some of whom become friends and some enemies, but all of whom long for the same thing—their freedom. As he watches some of his fellow prisoners fall into despair, Morris makes a discovery that suggests a possible way out. And, as a result, he and three accomplices set a plan in motion to do what has never been done before.

This movie is based on a true story.

Bible Passages

You may want to use these Bible passages during your movie discussion:

- John 8:36

  "So if the Son sets you free, you will be free indeed."

- 1 Corinthians 6:12

  " 'Everything is permissible for me'—but not everything is beneficial. 'Everything is permissible for me'—but I will not be mastered by anything."

- 1 Corinthians 8:9

  "Be careful, however, that the exercise of your freedom does not become a stumbling block to the weak."

- 1 Peter 2:16

  "Live as free men, but do not use your freedom as a cover-up for evil; live as servants of God."

DISCUSSION

After the movie, use some or all of these questions to discuss the spiritual themes in *Escape From Alcatraz*.

 Compare the perspectives of Doc and Frank Morris on the meaning and pursuit of freedom. How are they similar and how are they different? Which perspective do you identify with and why?

 Why do you think Doc's loss of painting privileges affected him the way it did? How do you think you would have responded if you were in that situation?

 Are freedom and submission to authority mutually exclusive? Why or why not?

 What does it mean to have freedom in Christ?

Just for Fun!

Got a few extra minutes? Quiz everyone on Clint Eastwood movie quotes. In which movie did his character say:

- *"What do you see when you're in the dark and the demons come?"*
  (In the Line of Fire)

- *"Are you gonna pull those pistols or whistle 'Dixie'?"*
  (The Outlaw Josey Wales)

- *"You've got to ask yourself a question: Do I feel lucky? Well, do ya, punk?"*
  (Dirty Harry)

- *"If you want a guarantee, buy a toaster."*
  (The Rookie)

- *"In this world there's two kinds of people, my friend. Those with loaded guns, and those who dig. You dig."*
  (The Good, the Bad, and the Ugly)

- *"Girlie, tough ain't enough."*
  (Million Dollar Baby)

- *"I ain't gonna be hitting you with my face."*
  (Every Which Way But Loose)

- *"NASA wants to send us into space."*
  (Space Cowboys)

- *"No forks."*
  (Escape From Alcatraz)

Describe a time when living out your spiritual freedom meant taking a risk. What was the result, and do you think the risk was worth it?

 For the few prisoners who successfully escape, what do you think their experience of freedom would be like from that time on? What lessons do you think we could take from their experience?

 What are things that might prevent a person from living freely—either spiritually or in relationships?

 What are some ways we can apply the lessons from this movie in our day-to-day lives?

PRAYER

Finish your time by praying together. First ask for prayer requests. Point out that, as in the movie, an important part of pursuing our freedom is partnering with other like-minded people—and one way we can do that is by partnering together in prayer. Then have everyone gather into groups of three or four to pray for each other—specifically praying that each would be able to apply lessons learned from watching and discussing *Escape From Alcatraz*. You may also want to consider having at least one person in each group agree to lead in prayer in case the other men are not comfortable praying out loud.

THE END

THE MOVIE

I, ROBOT

Genre: Sci-Fi Adventure   **Length:** 115 minutes   **Rating:** PG-13

Quick Plot: Even though robots are hard-wired not to hurt humans, Detective Del Spooner is convinced that one robot has committed murder.

Why This Movie Is Great for Guys: If you're a fan of action or science fiction, this movie won't disappoint you. It's a suspenseful, pulse-pounding thrill ride with an intelligent and thoughtful look at the heart of humanity.

 Note: This film is rated PG-13 for a lot of intense, stylized action, some violence, some bad language, and a shadowy, two-second shot of Will Smith's bare bum.

FOOD

In honor of Detective "Spooner," spoon foods:
I, Adobo (chili)
Sonny Corn Chips
Drinks (soda, iced tea, water)
G.G.'s Sweet Potato Pie
Rich Chocolaty Shakes

THE FOOD

Before your Dinner and a Movie event, talk to the guys about dividing the ingredients and supplies. Depending on the size of your group, some guys may need to bring more than one item.

What you'll need:

Names:

I, Adobo (chili) (serves 6)

1½ pounds ground beef _____

½ cup chopped onion _____

1 envelope chili seasoning mix _____

1 tablespoon adobo chili sauce _____

1 15-ounce can kidney beans _____

1 14½-ounce can diced tomatoes _____

grated cheddar cheese _____

1-2 bags corn chips _____

Rich Chocolaty Shakes (serves 6)

6 tablespoons powdered chocolate
drink mix _____

3-4 cups chocolate ice cream _____

5 cups milk _____

3 teaspoons vanilla extract _____

beverages (soda, iced tea, water) _____

G.G.'s Sweet Potato Pie
(recipe on page 104) _____

Easy Option Meal

If the guys in your group aren't into making food from scratch, pick up some pre-made deli or canned chili and a bag of chips. And instead of making fresh pie, grab a couple of pies (like pumpkin or pecan) from your grocer's bakery.

Since the main course is spoon-based, be sure not to forget the spoons! And since guys tend to forget things like napkins...don't forget the napkins!

1½ pounds ground beef
½ cup chopped onion
1 envelope chili seasoning mix
1 tablespoon adobo chili sauce

1 15-ounce can kidney beans (about 2½ ounces per person)
1 14½-ounce can diced tomatoes (about 2½ ounces per person)

Brown ground beef with onions over medium heat in large skillet. Mix in chili seasoning mix and adobo sauce, then stir in remaining ingredients. Bring to a boil. Reduce heat, cover, and simmer for 10 minutes. Top with grated cheese. Serves about 6.

Making Dinner Happen

You have the home-court advantage here, so make it easy on yourself and have a cooking plan in mind before the event (decide how you'll assign tasks for meal prep). Then, when guests arrive, distribute photocopied recipes and have everyone work together to get the food on the table.

Rich Chocolaty Shakes

3-4 cups chocolate ice cream
5 cups milk
3 teaspoons vanilla extract

6 tablespoons powdered chocolate drink mix

Put all ingredients into blender, and mix until smooth. Serves 6.

G.G.'s Sweet Potato Pie

2 cups cooked and mashed sweet potatoes
4 ounces butter, softened
2 cups sugar
1 can evaporated milk

3 eggs, beaten
1 teaspoon vanilla
1 teaspoon pumpkin pie spice
2 pie shells

Blend potatoes, butter, sugar, and evaporated milk. Mix in eggs, vanilla, and spice. Pour mixture into pie shells, and bake in preheated 350-degree oven for one hour (or until firm). Optional: Top with whipped cream. Each pie serves about 6.

GETTING READY FOR THE SHOW

TalkStarters

Use these questions to prompt discussions as you eat together:
• If you owned a robot that performed a regular task for you, what would you have it do?
• Think about movies you've seen with robots as part of the story. Which is your favorite movie robot? Why?
• Do you think we'll ever see the day when robots are an everyday part of our lives? Why or why not?
• Right now we're all choosing to eat this chili. Do you believe you're eating this food by your own free will, or do you believe God chose for you to eat this chili at this specific moment in time? Explain.

• If people truly do have "free will" to choose what they want to do, why do you think so many people try to discover God's will for their lives?

Will Smith Movie Quote Quiz

Name the movie that each of these Will Smith quotes comes from. Bonus points if you can name the movie's character!

1. "Life is not the amount of breaths you take, it's the moments that take your breath away."
2. "I hear you lost your swing. I guess we got to go find it."
3. "I have got to get me one of these!"
4. "That's it, no more Mr. Knife guy."
5. "I'm gonna give 1,000 dollars to the man who brings me Howard Cosell's toupee, dead or alive."
6. "You know the difference between you and me? I make this look good."
7. "You got a dream, you gotta protect it. People can't do something themselves, they wanna tell you that you can't do it. You want something? Go get it. Period."

Answers
1. Alex "Hitch" Hitchens in *Hitch*
2. Bagger Vance in *The Legend of Bagger Vance*
3. Captain Steven Hiller in *Independence Day*
4. James West in *Wild, Wild West*
5. Muhammed Ali in *Ali*
6. Agent J in *Men in Black*
7. Christopher Gardner in *The Pursuit of Happyness*

SHOWTIME!

The Pre-Show

Have everyone gather in the area where you'll show the movie. If you've just finished eating, provide a quick break for people to use the restroom.

When everyone has gathered, serve the G.G.'s Sweet Potato Pie and Rich Chocolaty Shakes to anyone who's ready for dessert. Don't forget the spoons!

THE SHOW

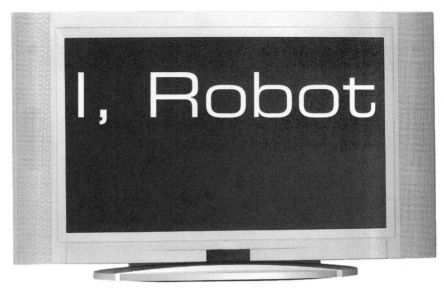

I, Robot

Genre: Sci-Fi Adventure

Length: 115 minutes

Rating: PG-13 for intense stylized action (including violence involving robots), occasional strong language, and a brief scene of partial nudity (an obscured, nonsexual, two-second shot of Will Smith's backside)

Plot: In the year 2035, robots have become as commonplace as cars and cell phones. And though robots are hard-wired not to hurt humans, Detective Del Spooner doesn't trust them. In fact, when he's called to investigate the death of a friend, a robot becomes his prime suspect.

But no one believes Spooner. Society has accepted the Three Laws of Robotics:

1. A robot may not harm a human or, by inaction, allow a human to come to harm.

2. A robot must obey orders given it by human beings except where such orders would conflict with the first law.

3. A robot must protect its own existence as long as such protection does not conflict with the first or second law.

In spite of these laws, Spooner is convinced that something sinister is afoot. Dr. Susan Calvin, a robot psychologist working for U.S. Robotics, helps Spooner in his investigation but is skeptical of his suspicions. But when Spooner is attacked by robots during the course of his investigation, he realizes the robot problem is much bigger than he ever imagined.

THE POST SHOW

Bible Passages

You may want to use these Bible passages during your movie discussion:

- Romans 9:18-22

  "Therefore God has mercy on whom he wants to have mercy, and he hardens whom he wants to harden. One of you will say to me: 'Then why does God still blame us? For who resists his will?' But who are you, O man, to talk back to God? 'Shall what is formed say to him who formed it, "Why did you make me like this?" ' Does not the potter have the right to make out of the same lump of clay some pottery for noble purposes and some for common use? What if God, choosing to show his wrath and make his power known, bore with great patience the objects of his wrath—prepared for destruction?"

- Galatians 5:1

  "It is for freedom that Christ has set us free. Stand firm, then, and do not let yourselves be burdened again by a yoke of slavery."

- 1 Peter 1:17

  "Since you call on a Father who judges each man's work impartially, live your lives as strangers here in reverent fear."

- Psalm 14:2-3

  "The Lord looks down from heaven on the sons of men to see if there are any who understand, any who seek God. All have turned aside, they have together become corrupt; there is no one who does good, not even one."

- Romans 12:2

  "Do not conform any longer to the pattern of this world, but be transformed by the renewing of your mind. Then you will be able to test and approve what God's will is—his good, pleasing and perfect will."

Just for Fun!

Got a few extra minutes? Quiz everyone on the following *I, Robot* movie quotes.

WHO SAID:

- *"You must be the dumbest smart person in the world."*
  (Del Spooner)

- *"You know, somehow, 'I told you so' just doesn't quite cut it."*
  (Del Spooner)

- *"Does believing you're the last sane man on the planet make you crazy? 'Cause if it does, maybe I am."*
  (Del Spooner)

- *"Are you being funny?"*
  (Dr. Susan Calvin)

- *"I think it would be better not to die, don't you?"*
  (Sonny)

- *"They all look like me. But none of them are me."*
  (Sonny)

- *"You cannot be trusted with your own survival."*
  (V.I.K.I.)

DISCUSSION

After the movie, use some or all of these questions to discuss the spiritual themes in *I, Robot*.

 What aspect of this movie stood out the most to you? Was there anything you'd have done differently if you'd been the director?

Imagine living in a robot-saturated world like 2035 Chicago (before the revelation that some of the robots were bad). What would you like about it? What would you dislike? How would it compare to the world we live in now?

 Why was Spooner distrustful of robots? How is this similar to the way we're sometimes distrustful of other people?

 When it comes to understanding the world around you, would you consider yourself more like Detective Spooner or Dr. Calvin? Why?

 How much free will did Sonny really have? Considering God's omniscience, how much free will do you think humans have?

 Can you relate with Sonny's desire to be unique? Why or why not?

 Sonny says, "I believe my father made me for a purpose." What purpose(s) do you believe God made you for?

 Spooner tells Sonny, "You'll have to find your way like the rest of us...That's what it means to be free." Do you agree with Spooner? Why or why not?

 In the end, Sonny is depicted on a hill with a bridge in the shape of a cross. In what ways was Sonny like or unlike Christ? In what ways is Sonny like or unlike us? In what ways is Christ like or unlike us?

PRAYER

Close your time together in prayer. Have each guy share one unique thing about himself, and then have each take turns praying for the guy to the left, thanking God for the unique way he made him.

THE END

Meet us for Dinner and a Movie: Adrenaline Rush

We're watching

BATMAN BEGINS

and eating food fit for a billionaire
(well, almost).

When: _____

Time: _____

Where: _____

_____

_____

RSVP: _____

Meet us for Dinner and a Movie: Adrenaline Rush

We're watching

STAR WARS

and eating from the Jedi's elite menu.

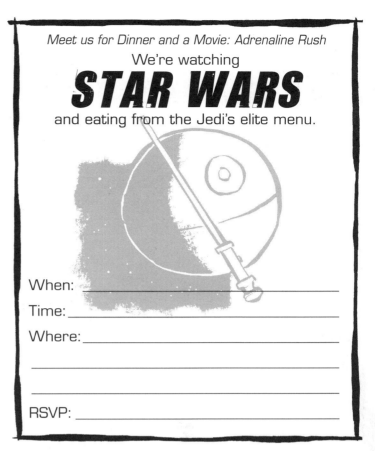

When: _____

Time: _____

Where: _____

_____

_____

RSVP: _____

Meet us for Dinner and a Movie: Adrenaline Rush

We're watching

MIRACLE

and eating a stadium vendor's best

When: _____

Time: _____

Where: _____

_____

_____

RSVP: _____

Meet us for Dinner and a Movie: Adrenaline Rush

We're watching

RAIDERS OF
THE LOST ARK

and eating a culinary treasure.

When: _____

Time: _____

Where: _____

_____

_____

RSVP: _____

Cut the invitations along dashed lines.

Meet us for Dinner and a Movie: Adrenaline Rush

We're watching

THE INCREDIBLES

and eating a superhero specialty.

When: _____

Time: _____

Where: _____

_____

_____

RSVP: _____

Meet us for Dinner and a Movie: Adrenaline Rush

We're watching

SIGNS

and eating Corn Surprise
(Surprise! It's corn.)

When: _____

Time: _____

Where: _____

_____

_____

RSVP: _____

Meet us for Dinner and a Movie: Adrenaline Rush

We're watching

GALAXY QUEST

and eating a meal suitable
for space explorers.

When: _____

Time: _____

Where: _____

_____

_____

RSVP: _____

Meet us for Dinner and a Movie: Adrenaline Rush

We're watching

THE EXORCISM OF EMILY ROSE

and eating comfort[ing] food.

When: _____

Time: _____

Where: _____

_____

_____

RSVP: _____

Cut the invitations along dashed lines.

Meet us for Dinner and a Movie: Adrenaline Rush

We're watching
APOLLO 13
and eating all-American fare.

When: _____

Time: _____

Where: _____

_____

_____

RSVP: _____

Meet us for Dinner and a Movie: Adrenaline Rush

We're watching
WHAT ABOUT BOB?
and eating food fit for a lakeside vacation.

When: _____

Time: _____

Where: _____

_____

_____

RSVP: _____

Meet us for Dinner and a Movie: Adrenaline Rush

We're watching
THE LORD OF THE RINGS: THE FELLOWSHIP OF THE RING
and eating what hobbits eat (what else?).

When: _____

Time: _____

Where: _____

_____

_____

RSVP: _____

Meet us for Dinner and a Movie: Adrenaline Rush

We're watching
THE BOURNE IDENTITY
and eating fisherman's fare.

When: _____

Time: _____

Where: _____

_____

_____

RSVP: _____

Cut the invitations along dashed lines.

We're watching

X-MEN

and enjoying a New York meal for mutants.

When: _____

Time: _____

Where: _____

_____

_____

RSVP: _____

We're watching

ESCAPE FROM ALCATRAZ

and eating something much better than prison food.

When: _____

Time: _____

Where: _____

_____

_____

RSVP: _____

We're watching

I, ROBOT

and eating a meal Detective Spooner would approve of.

When: _____

Time: _____

Where: _____

_____

_____

RSVP: _____

Cut the invitations along dashed lines.